Real Energy

Systems, Spirits, and
Substances to Heal, Change, and Grow

✦

Phaedra &
Isaac Bonewits

NEW PAGE BOOKS
A division of The Career Press, Inc.
Franklin Lakes, NJ

REAL ENERGY

EDITED BY KIRSTEN DALLEY

TYPESET BY EILEEN DOW MUNSON

Cover design by Scott Fray

Printed in the U.S.A. by Book-mart Press

To order this title, please call toll-free 1-800-CAREER-1 (NJ and Canada: 201-848-0310) to order using VISA or MasterCard, or for further information on books from Career Press.

The Career Press, Inc., 3 Tice Road, PO Box 687,
Franklin Lakes, NJ 07417
www.careerpress.com
www.newpagebooks.com

Library of Congress Cataloging-in-Publication Data

Bonewits, Phaedra, 1951-

Real energy : systems, spirits, and substances to heal, change, and grow / by Phaedra & Isaac Bonewits.

p. cm.

ISBN-13: 978-1-56414-904-6

ISBN-10: 1-56414-904-8

1. Magic. 2. Parapsychology. 3. Force and energy—Miscellanea. I. Bonewits, Philip Emmons Isaac. II. Title.

BF1611.B578 2007

133.4′3—dc22

2006103016

To our mothers,

Lillian Heyman and Jeanette Bonewits,

and our fathers,

Edward Heyman and Edwin Bonewits,

who proved that two Eds are better than one!

Contents

Introduction

What Do We Mean by "Real Energy"?

Energy is all around us. Everything we see, touch, and experience is made of energy. Solid matter seems to be composed of unmoving energies, while other kinds of matter, such as fire, light, or electricity, seem volatile. Energy is not just around us, it is us. Energy flows through us, becomes us, and is changed by us. Everything is energy, including us.

One of the things that Isaac likes to do late at night when he's trying to get to sleep is to watch the "energies" coming off his hands and feet. They usually appear to him as vague, colorless ripples in the air near his body parts, a little similar to the heat waves that rise into the air over asphalt on hot days. If he points a finger, Isaac can see a fat cone of something coming out of the end of that finger. With a little concentration, he can narrow that cone to a beam, which he can then sweep across the air in front of him, reaching several feet away from his hand.

Is he really doing or seeing anything, or is he "just imagining" that he is? This brings us to some core questions, not just for this book, but for all human philosophies and spiritual beliefs: What is the nature of reality? How can we define truth and falsehood? How do we judge the accuracy of our own perceptions? Because we are going to be discussing a wide variety of "stuff" that occultists, New Agers, Spiritualists, and Neo-Pagans call "energies," how can we possibly decide which are real and which are not?

dualism Mainstream Western culture has embraced a dualistic mindset in order to decide most such issues. In the monotheistic worldview in particular, everything that has ever existed in the past, that exists now, or is capable of existing in the future is evaluated according to whether it belongs to the Forces of Good or the Forces of Evil, while in the scientistic worldview, everything is evaluated according to whether it is 100 percent true or 100 percent false. Although both of these worldviews tend to think as the divisions between these concepts (true and false, good and evil) as concrete and immovable, it is also said that there is a dangerously "slippery slope" from goodness to the worst sorts of evil, or from shining truth into abject falsehood. *polarism* Chinese religions and philosophies, on the other hand, tend to think in terms of a concept we call "polarism" to decide questions about reality. In this, everything can be divided into oppositional pairs (yin and yang, male and female, and so on) that are thought to embrace, enhance, and support each other.[1] *pluralism* Tribal and other polytheistic cultures embrace "pluralism" as their touchstone of reality and ethics. In this worldview, reality is perceived as complex and multifaceted, with simple answers being treated only as shorthand for complicated issues.

According to the old saying, in the realm of the blind, the one-eyed man is king. History, however, tells us that in the realm of the blind, the one-eyed man is ignored, insulted, and, if he is unrepentant, sometimes even executed for heresy. Someone who is blind or deaf from birth lives in a different universe from the rest of us, and this person will, quite naturally, define his or her reality in a different way than the rest of us who can hear and see. Conversely, if most people were blind, a sighted person would have data available that would be confusing and even frightening to the rest. If this additional data enabled the sighted person was to do things that others couldn't do and couldn't explain, the sighted person would be seen as a threat.

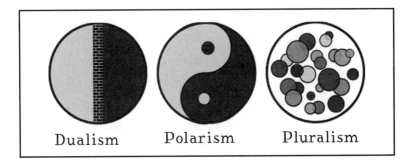

Figure 1: *Dueling paradigms.*

You can see this idea played out in the philosophical and theological realms by looking at how dualist, polarist, and pluralist systems handle information from outside their normal means and areas of knowledge. Dualists insist that new information or ideas must be fit into one of only two categories allowed to exist (true or false, rational or irrational, good or evil). If the information gets categorized as negative, the person or device presenting it may be ignored, denounced, or destroyed. Polarists will look at the data and ask, "Is there some way we can combine this idea with its opposite to get a better handle on it?" Pluralists will react to new information by saying, "Hmmm, that's interesting. I wonder what it means."

We, the authors, are pluralists, a mindset that the reader will find informs and infuses this entire work, as we attempt to discover how many different kinds of mystical, magical, psychic, or spiritual energies there may be, and what, if anything, they have to do with the energies studied by mainstream scientists. The reader may well wonder, however, just how qualified we are for this daunting task.

Our Backgrounds

Isaac has been writing about magic and mysticism for 35 years, ever since he graduated from the University of California–Berkeley in 1970 with a degree in magic and thaumaturgy. He published his first book, *Real Magic*, in 1971; it went on to become a classic beginners' text on the occult, and was eventually published in multiple editions (both authorized and pirated) around the world. In 1978, he published *Authentic Thaumaturgy*, a rewrite of *Real Magic* for players of fantasy role-playing games. This was one of the first books that attempted to describe the results of spells in terms of equations, mass, photons, temperature changes, and so on. Throughout the 70s, 80s, and 90s, Isaac was both studying and participating in the history and progress of the Earth Religions movement, resulting in the publication of such books as *The Pagan Man, Bonewits's Essential Guide to Witchcraft and Wicca*, and *Bonewits's Essential Guide to Druidism*. He was also actively studying and practicing various forms of Ceremonial Magic, liturgical design (which led to his book *Rites of Worship*, and the forthcoming *Neopagan Rites: A Guide to Creating Public Rituals that Work*), Voodoo and Santeria, Taoism and t'ai chi, and tantra and kundalini yoga. Through all these years of research and practice he has maintained that there is no innate conflict between the results of scientific research and the results of magical or mystical research—when they are compared fairly by people with a background in both the secular and the spiritual disciplines concerned, using appropriate measuring devices, and while keeping the appropriate levels of reality distinct.

Phaedra has been a practicing occultist for some 30 years, beginning with the study of Tarot and other divination systems in the 1970s. In the 80s and 90s she was active in Chicago's Neo-Pagan community, where she helped co-found Panthea Pagan Temple, which, in 1990, became the first Pagan congregation to affiliate with the Unitarian Universalist Association of Congregations (UUA). Near the end of the decade, she served as vice president of the continental board of the Covenant of Unitarian Universalist Pagans (CUUPS). Along the way, she has been initiated into Hermetic Magic and several forms of modern Witchcraft, and has close working relationships with practitioners of paths such as Ifa and Druidism (as regards the latter, mostly with the guy sitting next to her at his computer).

Phaedra's work with Hermetic Magic during the Chicago years was combined with a job as personal assistant to her High Priestess, who just happened to be an acupuncturist and body worker. Thus, she had the opportunity to experience first-hand the application of the energetic theories of oriental medicine, even serving as body model for a shiatsu course.

In the mid-90s, Phaedra owned and operated Explorations, the best little occult shop in downstate Illinois. As Peoria's finest purveyor of candles, oils, incenses, and rocks, she often had customers stand before the lavish display of crystals and ask, "Do these work?" Her standard reply was, "They are the most perfectly functional rocks you will ever find. Now, beyond that, what exactly are you expecting them to do?" It has been with that pragmatic approach that she has approached all her magical and energetic experiments.

It should be clear from all of this that neither one of us is a scientist in the mainstream sense, although Isaac likes to think of himself as an amateur anthropologist. Naturally, we knew that we were going to need considerable help, preferably from someone in the "hard" sciences. So we dialed a mystical 911 and called the Physics Police.

The Physics Police

Originally, the Physics Police consisted of two professional physicists, David Burwasser and Dr. York Dobyns, who were members of an online discussion group called CUUPS Café.[2] They were in the habit of jumping on sloppy science references made by the other participants, especially in matters related to physics. We asked Dave and York if they would be willing to give us fair warning when we might be straying too far afield from what mainstream Western science can support regarding the many real (and imagined) phenomena that mystics, magicians, Neo-Pagans, and New Agers like to call "energy." They also helped us to clarify our use of technical physics vocabulary. Dave was unfortunately unable to participate, but York was kind enough to grant our request.

York was educated at Ohio University (B.S., Physics, 1982) and Princeton University (M.A., Physics, 1985; Ph.D., Physics, 1987). He has published papers in *Astrophysical Journal Letters*, *Foundations of Physics*, *Annalen der Physik*, and the *Journal of Scientific Exploration*. Much of his career has been spent in the Princeton Engineering Anomalies Research program at Princeton University.

We also asked our friend Dr. Bill Seligman to join the force. Bill received his doctorate in particle physics from Columbia University in 1996. He was initiated into the Craft the same year. He tells us: "A physicist might assert that this was just a coincidence. A psychologist might point out that he spent years of work to achieve both goals. A witch might assert that this was his year for crossing the threshold." Bill continues to work in the world of high-energy physics. He also continues in his progress as a teacher of the Craft.

(Authors' note: Even though we presented much of the book to these two gentlemen for their comments, they should not be held responsible for any errors that may have crept in during later edits or galley proofing. All errors are entirely the responsibility of your humble authors.)

Overview of the Book

In Part I, we will look at the energy vocabularies and theories of both real scientists and real mystics over the last 3,000 years, in order to provide a theoretical and historical foundation to our efforts to see just how many kinds of mystical, magical, psychic, or spiritual "energies" really exist.

In Part II, we'll look at the energies that mystics use that appear to be rooted in the physical and metaphysical worlds in which they live. We'll begin with the cosmological concepts of the ancient Indo-Europeans and the medieval magicians and alchemists; take a quick tour of Chinese beliefs about the Tao and qi energies; look at various magical and psychic ideas about the mystical energies of the Earth and cosmos; and end with a discussion of rocks, plants, and animals as supposed sources of mystical energies.

In Part III, we'll explore the basic concepts of parapsychology and psychic research, look at the esoteric energies that different cultures have believed are generated by or attached to our (multiple) bodies, examine the main traditional categories of spiritual entities (nature spirits, ancestors, deities, and others), and discuss the types of spiritual energies to which these entities may be connected. Then we'll discuss various ways of generating and focusing mystical energies.

Get Some Exercise!

We've discovered that the toughest thing about writing about energy is the ineffable quality of energy itself. Language has its limitations. For example, we could describe electricity in very technical terms (in as much as electricity itself is understood— that is, not completely), but how do we describe the sensation of an electric shock? Well, it hurts, and you hope you don't ever get one again. Helpful, huh? In order to bring our point home, we could tell you to go pull a plug with wet hands (but this is not recommended—DO NOT try this at home!). Now, those who are foolish (or trusting) enough to try the experiment would certainly have a better idea of what an electrical shock feels like, but the skeptical (or sensible) reader, alas, is no better off than before.

So what are the poor authors to do? Exercise! Yes, we're working on increasing our average daily steps to 10,000 with the help of our trusty pedometers, plus stretching and, oh, wait— that's what we're doing to increase our *physical* energy. You, gentle reader, will get exercises centered on other kinds of energy here in this book. Along with our descriptions, you will find activities that may help you feel the energies we're describing.

We use the term "activities" very deliberately. Reading an exercise is not the same thing as doing an exercise. Energy exercises require active participation in order to have any benefit. Likewise, reading a ritual is not the same thing as doing a ritual. Take your time—don't expect shortcuts. Just because you might be doing an exercise a year from now in 20 seconds doesn't mean you don't have to take the 20 minutes to do it now. Somewhere in the back row, a hand is raised: "Other people ground and center in 20 seconds, so why should I take 20 minutes?" That's a fair question. The initial instructions we give you for this and other exercises may appear elaborate at first. As you practice, it will seem as though you are taking fewer steps to get to the same result. In fact, you are doing all the steps, just much more efficiently. You will have done them so often that they won't require your conscious attention, so you'll hardly notice doing them. Similar to a ballet dancer who once didn't know how to do a demi plié and who can now drop one on a dime, you will develop your skills with practice and repetition. Without this practice and repetition, you just won't progress.

Read through every exercise once completely before you begin. It won't be easy to do any exercise effectively while you are reading from a page. (This is especially difficult if you need to close your eyes.) If you are doing an exercise as a group, it is immensely helpful to have one person act as reader and lead the others through it. If you are doing an exercise by yourself with no one to read to you, consider doing a voice recording of the instructions that you can play back for yourself. If that is not feasible, read a section, pause, follow the instructions, then read the next section. Proceed until you have finished the exercise.

All of our exercises are examples, and are far from being the only "right" way to achieve the experiences we hope you will have. As befits the authors' pluralist worldviews, there may be many ways to achieve the same results; these just happen to be ones we think will work well for most folks, most of the time.

Now, onwards!

(Note: The exercises throughout this book assume the reader's ability to move, breathe, stand, sit, and so forth. You may therefore insert the modifier, "as well as you are able to do so," after the instructions for each exercise.)

Part
I

General
Background

Chapter 1

What Is Energy?

The Physical Vocabulary of Energy

Every discipline has its own special language and jargon. One word may have an extraordinarily precise meaning in one field, while the wider world may use the same word much more loosely. Energy is one of these words, and we'll be exploring it in this chapter.

Energy is a meaningful and widely used term in magical, mystical, and New Age practices, even if the real meaning is elusive. The magician, mystic, or energy worker uses the word fluidly and with wide application. To a physicist, however, it has a very precise meaning with which the physicist needs to be familiar in order to function and communicate in that field. In this chapter we'll look at the ways that physicists and other scientists use the term—often in ways that are baffling to those of us who aren't mathematicians. We'll also look at some of the odder ideas that physicists have been coming up with in recent years. We'll move on to the more mystical ways in which the word has been used in discourse throughout history, and end with a discussion of current metaphysical uses—and misuses—of language.

Energy comes from the Greek word *energia*, which means "active work." As physicists use it, work is far more than mowing your lawn or doing the dishes, though both of these certainly involve physical work. To a physicist, work means to make a change in something, usually by applying a force. A force, in turn, is any influence that may cause an object (a subatomic particle, a soccer ball, or a galaxy) to accelerate or slow down its motion in any direction. Forces seldom operate in isolation, but rather in combination with or against each other to produce net forces. Skiers, for example, find their acceleration down a hill to be a result of the many forces operating on them, such as gravity, the friction of the snow against their skis (converting velocity into heat), air resistance, and the conversion of their biochemical and neural energy to the task of swaying their bodies to cut down air friction and add to gravity's effects. Physicists in the early 21st century recognize four fundamental interactions that are often called (perhaps incorrectly) forces: gravitation, electromagnetism, the weak nuclear interaction, and the strong nuclear interaction. They believe that the ways in which particles and larger objects behave can be described and quantified by combinations of these four forces.

Power, on the other hand, though frequently confused with energy, is used by physicists to mean the amount of any given type of energy per a unit of time. For example, if you had two radio-controlled toy cars, the one that used more electricity would probably have more power and would be able to drive faster, climb steeper ramps, and/or pull more weight during a given timespan.

There are several different kinds of physical energy, each of which may, under various circumstances, convert to one or more of the others. Nuclear energy is the energy found inside atoms and among various subatomic particles. Chemical energy is the energy in the bonds that hold molecules (clusters of two or more atoms) together. Electrical and magnetic energy is the energy of an electrical or magnetic field. Radiant energy consists of electromagnetic waves, including light, x-rays, and radio. Thermal energy is simply heat (which isn't really all that simple). Kinetic energy is the energy of an object in motion, while potential energy is energy that is stored up in something and that could eventually be released.

In physics, a field is anything that takes on a particular value at every point in space; whether that space is empty or has something occupying it makes no difference. Physicists talk about gravity as a field because you can, in principle, state exactly how gravity is pulling on every particle of matter, and how it would pull on any particle that happened to be in a particular spot, even if there's nothing there just now. Ditto for electricity, magnetism, and the other fundamental forces. An electrical field is created wherever you have electrically charged particles—electrons, for example—that produce the electrical force that causes static electricity, which then pushes the flow of electrical charge or current through electrical conductors, such as wires. A magnetic field is produced by the motion of this current, which is where the magnetic force of magnets comes from. The term electromagnetism originates from the fact that the two forces are inextricably linked. A changing magnetic field creates an electric field, and a changing electric field generates a magnetic field. Neither of these forces would exist without the larger electromagnetic field, which fills all of space, exerts the electromagnetic force on electrically charged particles, and is changed by them in return. The electromagnetic field is present even in areas where its value is zero (meaning that it exerts no forces). You can grasp this idea by using the analogy of a pond's surface: if all of the ripples die away, leaving the pond perfectly flat and still, that doesn't mean the surface itself is gone.

Just as ripples in a pond are waves on the surface of the water, light and other electromagnetic radiations are now seen as waves—a propagating oscillatory disturbance—in the electromagnetic field, with the magnetic and electric parts in phase, or linked up, with each other, and at right angles to each other and the direction in which they are traveling, as shown in this illustration:

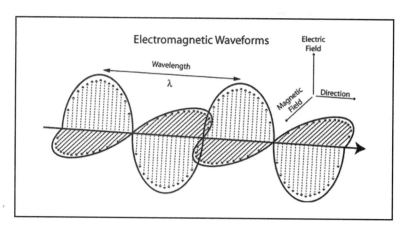

Figure 2: *Electromagnetic waveforms.*

Depending on how many waves are traveling a given distance, the wavelength and frequency are typically inversely proportional. Longer wavelengths mean a lower frequency (fewer of them) in a set distance; conversely, shorter wavelengths mean a higher frequency (more of them). Based on the upper and lower limits of wavelengths and frequencies observed by scientists, electromagnetic waves are placed on a spectrumthat includes radiant forces such as gamma rays, x-rays, microwaves, and radio waves, as seen here:

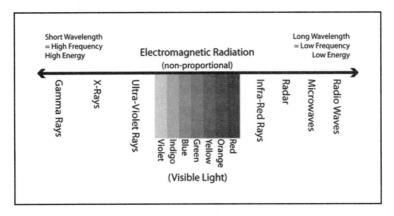

Figure 3: *The electromagnetic spectrum.*

Human beings can only see a small part of the electromagnetic spectrum—what we call the visible spectrum of the colors red through violet. The idea that just because we can't see something doesn't mean it's not there becomes very apparent here (as anyone who has had too many x-rays has found out, to their dismay).

Thermal energy is a measure of the total vibrational energy in all the molecules and atoms in any given object, and combines both the kinetic and the potential energy of the molecules' collisions. The kinetic energy is from the particles moving about randomly, while thermal potential energy comes from the electrons of the close atoms repelling each other through their electromagnetic force, thus bouncing away to collide with others. Thermal energy can also be thought of as a measure of the internal energy of a system (a steam engine, for example) when it is not doing anything to cause a change in temperature or pressure. If the thermal energy flows to another system it is called heat, and part of this flow can be converted into work. For example, heat can be used to boil water, which turns into steam, which runs a turbine, which generates electricity by spinning large magnets inside coils of wires.[1]

Kinetic energy explains why even small objects moving at high speed can cause enormous destruction. The forces necessary to accelerate and keep accelerating an object become momentum that can be difficult for anything in its path to stop, whether we're talking about an arrow going through a target or a bicyclist riding through a brick wall.

Potential energy is energy that can be released from something, such as a wound up spring, for example. Gravitational potential energy is the energy released by an object falling from a given height above the Earth, or the energy needed to raise that object to that height from the ground. Elastic potential energy is the sort that gets stored in a rubber band that has been pulled. Chemical potential energy is the kind locked up in the bonds between chemicals, before they are combined with other chemicals or subjected to forces such as heat. Rest mass energy is all the potential energy that could theoretically be released from an object if subjected to the right—or wrong—forces (this is what the "E" in Einstein's famous equation "$E=mc^2$" refers to, with the "m" representing the mass of an object at relative rest, and the "c" representing the speed of light in a vacuum).

Conservation of energy—in the sense that physicists today believe that energy within a closed system, including the energy temporarily locked up in matter, remains constant—is an idea that goes back to the late 17th century scientist Gottfried Wilhelm Leibniz (1646–1716), who called this characteristic the *vis viva*, or living force, of the system. (This should not be confused with the common term of a postulated life force, a special kind of energy that supposedly suffuses all life.[2] We'll talk more about this idea later in the chapter.) In the early 1800s, scientists began to call Leibniz's *vis viva* energy instead, at least in part because their definitions were starting to stress the idea of forces performing work, which sounded more scientific and fit within the dawning Industrial Age's worldview.

It should be remembered, however, that one kind of energy, such as matter, can often convert to another kind of energy once the system is no longer isolated; for example, this occurs when kinetic energy is partially turned into heat in the presence of friction (think meteors). Indeed, it was the various experiments measuring the heat generated by mechanical devices that led to the classification of heat itself as a form of energy. Remember also that totally isolated systems of matter and/or energy exist only in theory, and not in the mundane real world. If something were truly isolated and unreachable, we would have no way of perceiving it!

The Confusing Vocabulary of Quantum Theory

Most modern physicists believe that energy is always part of, or at least associated with, something moving in three or more dimensions at a particular velocity. This "something" is sometimes called a *quantum* (plural *quanta*), from the Latin for "how much?" This denotes an indivisible minimal unit of something that can be measured or quantized in the form of certain numerical values. For example, the quantum of light is the photon. In 1905, this concept led to something called wave/particle duality—the idea that something could function like a wave of energy in some circumstances, and a particle or speck of matter in others. It also led to the creation of quantum mechanics (these are not the people who fix broken quanta) as the field of study that deals with the behavior of very small phenomena such as atoms and their subatomic waves/particles, some of which required the invention of new descriptive (and often poetic) terms such as "charm" and "strangeness," their meanings understood only by initiates of the mysteries. As odd and foreign as some of these ideas may seem to non-physicists, quantum mechanics is now pretty much the rock-bottom, core approach to the physics taught and learned by all mainstream physicists. Every other type of modern physics has to be able to reconcile its theories and observations with those of quantum mechanics, just as its ideas had to be reconciled with the earlier theories of classical mechanics. Quantum mechanics is the conceptual toolbox used to construct quantum field theory and quantum physics in general, which, along with general relativity, is one of the pillars of modern physics.

There is absolutely no way that we can explain the basics of modern quantum theories or particle physics in a book such as this—we're not physicists, and we can't claim an in-depth understanding of these theories. As we will see later in this chapter, every generation of mystics and metaphysicians tries to explain what it is doing in terms of what is considered cutting-edge science at that time. Late 20th and early 21st century physicists have given New Agers and others plenty of interesting concepts to play with, many of which are eerily similar to earlier metaphysical theories, and a few of which have been appropriated or stolen (as some physicists would contend) to say things their originators never intended. Less stuffy physicists, however, are not bothered by this linguistic borrowing. As York Dobyns says:

The attitude that other communities are "hijacking" our technical jargon is in my opinion one of the most regrettable vices of the physics community. For me to be charged with a crime would imply absolutely nothing about my personal excess or deficit of electrons. The gravity of the charges would be completely irrelevant to their effect on spacetime curvature, except insofar as it might increase the mass of legal briefs and affidavits sharing the courtroom with me. The colors of quarks are quite unrelated to anything the eye can see, nor will their flavors be found in any eatery.

We physicists have been absolutely shameless about grabbing ordinary words and turning them into technical jargon. We have no right to complain, or invoke loaded terms like "hijacking," when a different community of specialists does the same, not even if it's a word one of us coined (such as "energy"). The colloquial meaning of "energy" derives from and is closely related to its original technical meaning, and the technical meaning among Pagan or New Age practitioners derives from the colloquial meaning in a completely different direction. Physicists who complain about misuse of the word are themselves simply missing the point.[3]

Bill Seligman adds:

One of the main causes of confusion in discussions between scientists and practitioners of magic is that they use words differently. Scientists attempt (with varying degrees of success) to establish precise definitions of the terms they use. A recent example of this was the definition applied to the word "planet" in August 2006 by the

International Astronomical Union (IAU); it relegated Pluto to the status of "dwarf planet."

I was taught that a witch walks between the worlds, and that among those worlds are the fuzzy and ever-changing meaning of words. Words have power; for more on this, see Isaac's *Real Magic*. No magical worker was surprised that some people objected to the IAU's decision. On the purely scientific level, Pluto is a label we've given to a chunk of rock far off in the solar system. On the personal level, we have developed images associated with Pluto with which a magician would cheerfully make use. We've been taught for years that there were nine planets, and we experienced a challenge to our personal pictures of the universe; Pluto is Roman name for the Greek god Hades, the ruler of the Underworld, and we can't expect him to be happy if he's "dwarfed."

The use by scientists of words in vernacular makes things more complex for the layperson, and more of a delight for the magician.

The other day I had to explain to someone that just because physicists use the "Uncertainty Principle" to describe the behavior of subatomic particles did not mean that the particles themselves were "uncertain" in any way.[4] When I'm at work, a coworker can talk to me about the different energy levels of a B-meson, and her different energy levels before and after her first cup of coffee of the day, using the same words to describe two different concepts (it might suit a magician to picture B-mesons drinking cups of coffee).

The way I manage this, as a physicist and a witch, is to recognize (in the words taught to me by my High Priestess) that "a witch has a foot in both worlds." One learns when to use words with precision, and when to swim among liquid multiple meanings within language.[5]

Whatever your opinion about "hijacking" vocabulary, we're going to do the best we can in the pages that follow to clarify how we, and the people we are discussing, use our technical terms. In defense of some of our more creative interpreters of terminology in the mystical, magical, Neo-Pagan, and New Age movements, however, we will point out that a number of legitimate physicists with particular theological or philosophical axes to grind have taken various philosophical concepts (interpretations) connected with the results (observations) of quantum physics experiments, and come to all sorts of interesting (and sometimes just plain weird) conclusions in popular books, some of which were then read and misinterpreted by enthusiastic energy workers. Therefore, rather than sort out all the physics terminology that has been abused by the true believers of various sects, we will just mention the worst victims—terms that are often misunderstood by the general public as well as people with a more mystical bent. Think of it as our effort to prevent the creation of more "fluffy bunny physicists."

The uncertainty principle does not mean that nothing can ever be known for sure in any blanket sense. It means that when measuring the location of subatomic particles, such as electrons in orbit around an atom's center, all we can actually measure is the cloud of probabilities of it being somewhere within a certain radius of a sphere. More specifically, we can measure (at least in theory) *either* the position *or* the momentum of a particle or wave with total precision, but never both characteristics at the same time—in part because as the precision of the position measurement increases, the precision of the momentum measurement decreases, and vice versa. In fact, the wave/particle duality we mentioned earlier means that every so-called particle, due to its inherently wavelike aspects, can't have a precise momentum and a precise location at the same time—an irreducible uncertainty is built into the thing we're measuring, and can't be gotten around by designing a more advanced instrument. This means that all scientific predictions based on quantum mechanics are probabilistic, not absolute, which many physicists in the first half of the 20th century, especially Albert Einstein, found upsetting.

God does not play dice.

One interesting consequence of such uncertainty is the concept of the multiverse. This holds that all the possibilities described by quantum theory—for example, that a burst of radiation could have gone off in hundreds of different directions—really occur in parallel universes that we can never directly observe. This idea eventually led to science fiction authors suggesting that every human decision creates two or more universes in which each possible variation of the decision was made. Some mystical authors then took the idea from either the physicists or the sci-fi writers, and ran off with it in multiple (infinite?) directions. Physicists, however, would insist that such parallel universes would be very much like our own, with identical laws of nature, and would be impossible to communicate with, so they cannot be equated with the mystical concepts of the Otherworld or astral planes.

Quantum entanglement refers to situations in which the quantum states (the total measured characteristics) of two or more objects—for example, matter or energy systems—have to be described in terms of each other. While this describes most interactions between particles, it also implies that changing one will change the other, even if they are separated by vast distances.

Einstein called this "spooky action at a distance," and hated the idea. Physicists are quick to say that this can't be used to transmit information faster than light; however, the equations for all of this made Isaac's head hurt, so we can't tell you why this is so, other than citing the theory that nothing, not even information, is able to travel faster than the speed of light. Apparently it will be a while before the idea of quantum entanglement can be used for real teleportation, even though some physicists use the term. Officer York of the Physics Police offers this "quick primer on entanglement (no equations necessary)":

> Although QM [quantum mechanics] says that any particles that have ever interacted are entangled, under most circumstances the entanglement is restricted to a quantity called the "phase" which cannot be observed by any measurement. The exception occurs when the entangled particles are carefully isolated from external interactions until you make just one measurement on each of them. That measurement "breaks" the entanglement (i.e. kicks it down into those unobservable phase values again) but, by comparing the measurements after the fact, the crew at detectors A and B can verify that the particles were related to each other in a particular way. The kicker is that no manipulation performed at A can change the statistics of particles seen at B (nor vice versa), and the statistics are all you have to go on until you can compare the detailed records at A and B, transmitted by some mundane communications channel. Thus, no signaling. Actually, some recent work hints that the no-signaling theorems just might be wrong, but trying to explain that does get us into extremely hairy math.

A quantum field does not refer to what fans of *Star Trek* might call subspace, but rather to the idea that the well-known fields we've already talked about are themselves quantum objects: the field values at every point obey an uncertainty principle and function according to the rules of quantum mechanics. Our entire solar system, for example, exists within several quantum fields (one of which may or may not be gravitational) centered on the sun.

Dark matter refers to invisible matter—that is, matter that doesn't seem to interact with EM (electromagnetic) fields and so can't be detected with EM instruments. Physicists infer its existence from its gravitational effects on visible matter. According to a report from NASA released on August 21, 2006, analysis of a gigantic collision of two clusters of galaxies has shown that the passage of the smaller through the larger cluster ripped dark matter apart from regular matter, thus proving its existence. Current astrophysics holds that most of the matter in the universe may be this kind of dark matter. There is even dark energy, which supposedly fills the universe and has strong negative pressure that seems to act in opposition to gravity. There are two proposed forms for dark energy: the cosmological constant or energy density of empty space (which supposedly does not change over time or space); and quintessence (an old alchemical term), a dynamic field whose energy density can vary in time and space. Both of these ideas are offered to explain why the universe appears to be currently expanding at an accelerating rate, after slowing down from the original Big Bang. As of 2006, estimates are that 5 percent of the universe is made of regular matter, 25 percent is dark matter, and 70 percent is dark energy.[6] We sincerely doubt that invisible matter and energy will have much to do with the mystical concepts of astral planes and Otherworlds; however, they may be connected to how some of the active psychic talents work, and may eventualy lead to a revival of the concept of the ether.

We'll return to these and other concepts of mainstream physics at various points throughout this book. In the meantime, let's take a look at the vocabulary of metaphysics.

Metaphysical Vocabulary: Ancient Times Through the 17th Century

Metaphysics is a term used by philosophers to refer to that branch of philosophy that discusses questions of ultimate meaning, questions such as "what is reality," "what is the nature of the world," "are there deities and what are they like," and "what is the meaning of life, the universe, and everything?" It has also been used for a few centuries to describe the study of things that are beyond (*meta-*) normal physics, such as magic, mysticism, psychic phenomena, and fundamental questions about *What the Bleep Do We Know?* Metaphysics, in all of its manifold meanings, is something that people have been pondering and participating in for thousands of years, however informally. In this chapter we'll take a look at the different words people have used to label the metaphysical energies they believe they have come into contact with.

As physicists and cosmologists have discovered, the further away something is from being readily observed and understood, the looser and more opaque the language gets—"charmed particles exhibiting strangeness" indeed! Not surprisingly, metaphysical vocabulary can get as loose as a pack of ferrets in a daycare center. Every generation of clergy, healers, magicians, diviners, spiritualists, parapsychologists, Neo-Pagans, and various New Age energy workers has tried to describe the powerful yet invisible energies they perceived and attempted to control. Each has used its own preferred vocabulary, informed by how they conceived of the phenomena involved. In each case, metaphors rooted first in traditional knowledge, then in esoteric wisdom known only to a few, then in science and technology, were the preferred tools used to explain the unexplainable. Sometimes the choice of language represented an appeal to intellectual authority figures, and sometimes it was a reflection of the fact that the energy workers themselves were their culture's authority figures—loosely equivalent to modern doctors, scientists, and philosophers. It is very important to remember that the thousands (millions?) of people involved in these intellectual processes were not stupid—most were, by the standards of their times and places, considered pretty darned smart.

Among the ancient peoples of the world, and for thousands of years around the globe, these various mystical energies were usually thought of as spiritual in the sense that they were thought to involve deities, ancestors, nature spirits, or other entities rooted in animism ("everything is alive"), pantheism ("the gods are all and in all"), and/or panentheism ("the gods are immanent as well as transcendent"). As we will see, metaphysical terms that involve universal or cosmic energies can easily blur into these spirit-based terms.

The personification of various forces seemed logical to most ancient cultures because they saw the universe as filled with life. Because they all knew they had ancestors, and hoped to have descendents as well, the fact that the ancestors didn't seem to be visible at any given moment didn't necessarily mean they weren't around somewhere, perhaps in a spirit world that overlapped with or could somehow communicate with the ordinary or mundane world. Archeology appears to provide evidence that our prehistoric predecessors believed in various kinds of spirits as far back as tens of thousands of years ago. We know through the archeology of more recent times, as well as through history, mythology, and linguistics, that people all over the world for at least the last 7,000 years worshipped gods and goddesses, honored their ancestors, gave offerings to spirits associated with both wild nature and civilized inventions, and had a few entities here and there that didn't fit into neat, modern categories, but who were nonetheless seen as important.

When a priestess, bard, shaman, medicine woman, witch doctor, Druid, or any other sort of healer or magician did what they did, they very often invoked the aid of spirits, whether major deities or minor sprites. Indeed, magic, mysticism, and healing were often seen by the ancients as a matter of developing spiritual communication skills with the appropriate entities, rather than as the manipulation of inanimate natural forces. Gradually they learned that certain objects, herbs, substances, arts, and psychological techniques seemed to have special properties that made their work easier and more reliable. Today we can smugly explain the results of their efforts as "natural" and predictable, and brought about merely through biology (medicines, psychedelics), plus a little rudimentary human (and animal) psychology and hypnosis. Yet examples of primitive superstition working effectively still exist today—something that modern scholars can't explain away no matter how hard they try. Could it be that the magical, spiritual, artistic, and psychological tools that the ancients used worked in more than just one way, and that the 19th-century rationalist explanations we still cling to today are just too simplistic?

Classical Greek and Roman philosophers, mystics, magicians, and clergy, as well as the later medieval ceremonial or goetic magicians, had an energy vocabulary that included sympathies (things that went well together, such as certain herbs and certain illnesses or body parts), powers (abilities to produce strong effects), and virtues (useful qualities) to describe the quasi-physical characteristics of mostly natural objects and phenomena. Many also believed that what they did could involve the participation of the spirits, and/or the physical and spiritual aspects of the four Elements (Air, Earth, Fire, and Water), first delineated by the Greek philosopher Empedocles. These were very different from the Chinese Elements in that they were thought of as the non-living parts from which all physical reality was constructed.

Qi
v
prana

The ancient Chinese embraced the concept of a life force or spiritual energy that was distributed throughout the cosmos and flowed through all living things. This force was called *qi* or *chi* (later known in Japan as *ki*). It is most often translated into English as "breath," perhaps relating it historically or metaphorically with the Indian concept of *prana*. Chinese scholars asserted that qi flowed along channels in the body, called *meridians* in English, which later became the focal points of acupuncture and acupressure. Different schools of Chinese thought have argued about whether qi comes from matter or matter comes from qi, or whether matter and qi are distinct but connected phenomena. Most Chinese martial arts involve the use of qi, including ways of stimulating its production and channeling its flow outside of the warrior's body through weapons (or even just the air) and into one's opponents. Many Chinese philosophers, past and present, seem to think that qi is just a metaphor, while others contend that it is a literal form of energy somehow connected to the forms of energy known by Western scientists, such as bioelectricity. The Chinese five Elements (Earth, Water, Fire, Wood, and Metal), while often equated to the Greek or Western Elements (Earth, Water, Air, Fire, and Spirit), actually represent phases of qi, and not the basic building blocks from which matter and energy are constructed (see Chapter 5 for more on the Chinese approach to understanding qi, and Chapter 3 for more on the Western Elements).

In India, the Brahmin caste of clergy and other intellectuals developed the various mystical systems known as *yogas*. The word yoga comes from a Sanskrit root meaning "yoke," which carries the connotation of discipline. There are many yogas, including hatha (physical) yoga, bakti (devotional) yoga, raja (intellectual) yoga, and Tantric (sexual) yoga. Tantric yoga also works with a special kind of energy called *kundalini*, which is believed to reside at the base of the spine and be able to climb, like a serpent, up the spine to the top of the head, where it gives the yogi transcendental bliss. Experienced yogis can develop *siddis*, or special abilities such as telepathy, clairvoyance, and healing. Basic to all yogas is the concept of *prana*, a Sanskrit word meaning "breath," which is understood to be both the life force present in all living beings, and a vital energy distributed throughout the universe and necessary for its processes. Because of this, breathing exercises became primary tools in all the yogic systems. There are patterns in these conceptualizations that we will see repeated in the energy vocabularies of many other traditions.

The yogic systems also describe pathways through the body—similar to the Chinese meridians through which qi was thought to flow—called *nadi*. In addition, Hindu esoteric physiology held that there were centers of whirling energy called *chakras* ("wheels") along the spine and elsewhere, each of which had its own special kind of energy associated with such concepts and activities as sexuality, power, feelings, communication, clairvoyance, and so on (see Chapter 8 for more on chakras and Tantra).

In ancient Polynesia, Melanesia, and Micronesia, the term *mana* was used to refer to the many different sorts of energy that modern westerners might variously call spiritual, psychic, magical, providential, artistic, sexual, or physiological. Its original meaning may have had connotations of respect or charisma—the sense of awe that certain people, places, and things could inspire in observers—as well as the moral obligations of responsibility and purity that such power in humans entailed. Here again, mana was seen as something that filled much (if not all) of the rest of the world and kept living things alive.

Mana became part of the metaphysical vocabulary of westerners through two sources—the scholarly writings of anthropologists about oceanic cultures, and the not-so-scholarly writings (okay, probably mostly invented stuff) published by Max Freedom Long in the middle of the 20th century. Nonetheless, because it has so many possible uses, mana became one of Isaac's favorite magical terms.

During the European Middle Ages and the Renaissance, and after the Paleo-Pagan clergy, healers, bards, and other users of mystical energies had been suppressed throughout Christendom and the Islamic lands, people who became known as ceremonial or goetic magicians appropriated the idea of the four Elements (adding a fifth one for Spirit), as well as other natural concepts of the Greeks and Romans. For their own safety, they replaced the Pagan spirits with various aspects of the one official deity, with addition of angels, demons, daemons, and Elementals. During the 17th and 18th centuries, magicians prided themselves on being natural philosophers (what we would call scientists) and dropped most of the spirit-dependent metaphors.

Metaphysical Vocabulary: The 18th Through the 20th Centuries

Franz Mesmer (1734–1815) invented a trance-inducing and healing technique (now called mesmerism) that used something he called animal magnetism. He believed that this magnetism was generated by humans and animals (from the Latin *animus*, or breath) that breathed. He distinguished it from mineral magnetism (the ordinary kind exhibited by magnetized iron or other metallic substances), as well as from planetary and cosmic magnetism (probably what we would call gravity and other astrological influences). Mesmer also believed that there was a magnetic fluid that animal bodies generated, and that it was possible to manipulate that fluid both internally and externally. The fact that he considered breath to be an important defining characteristic of this energy might very well link it with Indian prana and Chinese qi. By the middle of the 20th century, Mesmer's physical and psychological techniques were supplanted by the purely psychological methods of hypnotism, and later, neurolinguistic programming, leaving all the metaphysical aspects of his work ignored. But before that happened, his work was highly influential for the generations of scientists looking for connections between consciousness, biology, and electromagnetic energy.

Karl von Reichenbach (1788–1869) was an early, mainstream scientist specializing in chemistry, metallurgy, and biology, as well as philosophy. In 1844 he began research into the physiological effects of magnets and crystals. Reichenbach became convinced that there were specific non-physical energies active in living organisms and absent in all non-living matter. He named this energy *od*, or the *odic force*, after the Norse deity Odin. He believed that the odic force could have a positive or negative flux or flow, and that it could be seen as dark clouds or glowing lights. He spent years working with psychics and other sensitive (artistic, neurotic, feeble-minded, or insane, in modern parlance) individuals attempting to view the odic force in and around bodies and shining from hands or faces. Because many of Reichenbach's experiments involved people sitting in dark rooms and trying to see and/or produce glowing lights of odic force from their hands, Isaac finds himself wondering if the glow he himself has managed to produce and observe might be this sort of energy, rather than anything necessarily psychic or magical (or merely retinal afterimages).

In 1849, Reichenbach published his ideas in a book titled *Researches on Magnetism, Electricity, Heat, Light Crystalization and Chemical Attraction in Relation to the Vital Force* (translated from the German). Despite the fact that he was a distinguished scientist and a member of the Prussian Academy of Sciences, the existing dualistic bias in the scientific community rejected anything evenly remotely psychic or paranormal, which meant that his work was ignored by the mainstream. It was, however, to become influential among occultists, mystics, and philosophers. His belief that the odic force could be stored in crystals, for example, may have been the seed from which some of the modern New Age interest in crystals has grown. (And alas, it is upon this modern relationship that the reputation of this scientific detective falls.)

Much of Reichenbach's influence was to come through a novel by Sir Edward Bulwer-Lytton (1803–1873) titled *Vril, The Power of the Coming Race*, published in 1871. In this early science fiction novel, the protagonist enters an underground world of superhuman people who run their entire civilization and culture through the use of a mysterious energy called vril. As Bulwer-Lytton put it in his rolling Victorian language:

These subterranean philosophers assert that, by one operation of vril, which Faraday [Michael Faraday, the pioneering scientist of electromagnetism and electro-chemistry] would perhaps call "atmospheric magnetism," they can influence the variations of temperature—in plain words, the weather; that by other operations, akin to those ascribed to mesmerism, electro-biology, odic force, etc., but applied scientifically through vril conductors, they can exercise influence over minds, and bodies animal and vegetable, to an extent not surpassed in the romances of our mystics. To all such agencies they give the common name of vril.

Zee [the protagonist's guide] asked me if, in my world, it was not known that all the faculties of the mind could be quickened to a degree unknown in the waking state, by trance or vision, in which the thoughts of one brain could be transmitted to another, and knowledge be thus rapidly interchanged. I replied, that there were among us stories told of such trance or vision, and that I had heard much and seen something of the mode in which they were artificially effected, as in mesmeric clairvoyance; but that these practices had fallen much into disuse or contempt, partly because of the gross impostures to which they had been made subservient, and partly because, even where the effects upon certain abnormal constitutions were genuinely produced, the effects, when fairly examined and analyzed, were very unsatisfactory—not to be relied upon for any systematic truthfulness or any practical purpose, and rendered very mischievous to credulous persons by the superstitions they tended to produce.

Zee received my answers with much benignant attention, and said that similar instances of abuse and credulity had been familiar to their own scientific experience in the infancy of their knowledge, and while the properties of vril were misapprehended, but that she reserved further discussion on this subject till I was more fitted to enter into it. She contented herself with adding, that it was through the agency of vril, while I had been placed in the state of trance, that I had been made acquainted with the rudiments of their language; and that she and her father, who, alone of the family, took the pains to watch the experiment, had acquired a greater proportionate knowledge of my language than I of their own; partly because my language was much simpler than theirs, comprising far less of complex ideas; and partly because their organization was, by hereditary culture, much more ductile and more readily capable of acquiring knowledge than mine. At this I secretly demurred; and having had, in the course of a practical life, to sharpen my wits, whether at home or in travel, I could not allow that my cerebral organization could possibly be duller than that of people who had lived all their lives by lamplight. However, while I was thus thinking, Zee quietly pointed her forefinger at my forehead and sent me to sleep.

He should have known better than to argue with a priestess! It's entirely possible that the author only wanted to have a *deus ex machina* power in his tale that could be credited with performing all the wonders, both mystical and mundane, he wished to describe. Or he may have felt that there really was something that combined the magnetically connected odic forces of Baron von Reichenbach and the energies used by mediums and clairvoyants of his time. Either way, as he presented it, vril was a universal energy with electrical, magnetic, luminescent, antigravitational, mesmeric, and telepathic properties. To put it in modern terms, the inhabitants of his underground world had discovered a unified field theory, in which any form of energy could be converted into another through a combination of physical devices and mental powers developed through genetic engineering and lifelong training.

While he may have been influenced by the earlier *Journey to the Center of the Earth*, by Jules Verne (first published in French in 1864), Bulwer-Lytton's vivid imaginings arguably had a greater influence on later science fiction writers, occultists, mystics, Atlantean researchers, and ufologists (researchers of UFOs, or unidentified flying objects) than Verne's did.

Phineas T. Quimby (1802–1866) devised a system of healing that taught that all illness was rooted in ideas. According to him, people who weren't very adept at clear thinking, especially if they had been raised in a traditional Christian religious environment, merely needed to have their mental conflicts straightened out in order to be cured. He believed that the mind and body were separate but connected, and that one could influence the other. The techniques he originally used were solely intellectual (and could actually be considered proto-psychological therapy), and involved no physical or even quasi-physical energies. In 1838, he became involved in the study of mesmerism, and began combining it with his intellectual persuasion techniques, supposedly curing thousands of people over the course of his career. Among his students were some of the founders of the New Thought movement, as well as the founder of Christian Science, Mary Baker Eddy.

From the mid-19th century through the mid-20th century, Spiritualism had a profound effect on the way mystical energies were commonly understood. Although the movement itself was completely decentralized, there were a number of people who could be considered its founders. Spiritualism was a hodgepodge of Mesmer's hypnotic methods for inducing trances, Emanuel Swedenborg's mystical writings about conversations with spirits, liberal Christian theology, folk beliefs regarding ghosts and hauntings, early feminism, and a variety of mystical ideas taken from Theosophy. Spiritualism's primary focus was communicating with the dead through the "medium" of a person who would be able to both attract and control them, often through being partially or totally possessed by the real or alleged spirits. Women were prominent leaders throughout its history (as they were in Theosophy); interestingly, the spirits being channeled through the mediums often spoke out against slavery and for women's rights.

While early Spiritualism had little in the way of an organized theology, one of its offshoots, Spiritism, became a major religion in South America, as it still is today. Spiritism was created by the French scholar H. L. D. Rivail, a.k.a. Allan Kardec (1804–1869), who wrote *The Spirits' Book*, *The Book on Mediums*, and several other works. Meanwhile, although most Spiritualists in America and Europe attended liberal Christian churches with such folks as the Quakers, the Unitarians, and the Universalists, many were also agnostics. Quite a few independent Spiritualist Churches were organized over the decades, gradually linking up into unions and associations, and eventually splitting into two major categories—the Christian Spiritualists, and everybody else. While most of the mediums referred vaguely to certain psychic or spiritual energies being used in their trances, the term *ectoplasm* became closely associated with Spiritualism. This was thought of as a dense form of life force, bio-energy, or etheric energy that could be shaped mentally by mediums or spirits to move objects or make spirits visible.

Theosophy was founded in 1875 by a world-traveling psychic and medium named Helena Petrovna Blavatsky (1831–1891) and others. It was a form of universalist religion and philosophy that rejected traditional public or "exoteric" spiritual teachings in favor of secret or "esoteric" ones, some of which Blavatsky claimed to have learned from Mahatmas ("great spirits") in Tibet. In order to create her system, she cheerfully plundered (and garbled) ancient Greek, Roman, and Egyptian religions, Hinduism, Buddhism, Tibetan Bon, Islam, Christianity, Western Ceremonial Magic, the Christian Cabala, and other religions and philosophies for her core concepts, then tossed in a number of ideas from the scientific arena. She published many of her theories and claims—which some say were plagiarized outrageously—in *Isis Unveiled* in 1877, and *The Secret Doctrine* in 1888. These and her later writings, as well as those by others in the Theosophical Society, had a profound effect on the entire Western occult and metaphysical community then existing, as well as the New Thought movement yet to come. Her insistence that science and "true" religion were not incompatible gave rise to the idea that religions and philosophies ought to evolve *with* scientific knowledge, rather than fight *against* it.

Blavatsky and her followers described a system of invisible planes of matter and energy, using the metaphor that each was at a higher vibration than the one before (this may have been taken from the Spiritists). These included the earth plane of ordinary physicality, as well as the etheric, astral, mental, and causal planes, all arranged in an ascending hierarchy of power. These planes were said to interpenetrate each other, so changes caused by a magician or mystic upon a higher plane could effect similar changes in the ones below.

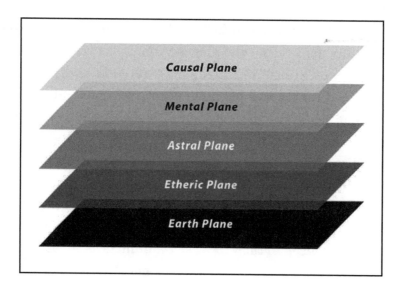

Figure 4: *The Theosophical vibratory planes in a vertical orientation.*

These planes can also be seen as overlapping spheres, as shown in Figure 5 on page 49. Sometimes seeing them as nested, one within the other, as shown in Figure 6, can also be helpful.

Similar names and concepts are used by modern psychic healers and energy workers to describe nested layers of energy

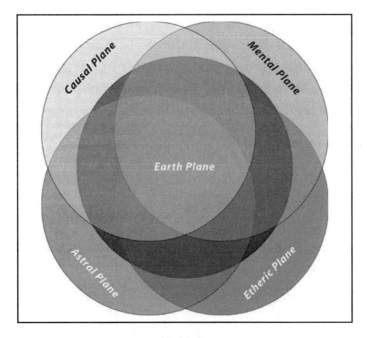

Figure 5: *The planes as overlapping vibratory spheres.*

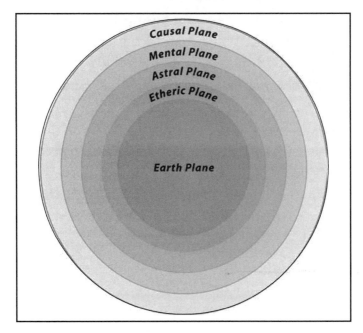

Figure 6: *The planes as nested vibratory spheres.*

fields in and around human and animal bodies, in part because Blavatsky's terms were translations of conflicting Hindu and Chinese esoteric physiological vocabulary. The various names for the different planes and their subcategories can be confusing because there are so many of them.

Christian Science, founded by Mary Baker Eddy (1821–1910), started with Quimby's theories and combined them with Eddy's liberal interpretations of the Christian Bible. One of the things about Quimby that had annoyed Eddy was his dismissal of most traditional Christian doctrines; in their conservative dogmatic forms at least, Quimby saw them as contributors to mental illness. Eddy's response was that the Biblical Christ needed to be seen as having been primarily a healer who used parables and metaphors to teach the unreality of all illness. While modern experts on hypnosis, neurolinguistic programming, and other psychological reprogramming methods can and do make the argument that listening to long boring lectures can induce a trance state among attendees at Christian Science meetings (they always did with Isaac), Eddy herself always distinguished between what she was teaching on one hand, and hypnotism or mesmerism on the other. She used the term "animal magnetism," almost always modified with the word "malicious," only to refer to the surreptitious mental influences that other people could, consciously or unconsciously, inflict upon others. This attitude apparently had something to do with the fact that Quimby may have abused Eddy in various ways while she was in a trance.[7]

Emma Curtis Hopkins (1849–1925) was a student of Eddy's, and was an influential figure in Christian Science until she was kicked out by Eddy. Hopkins became a theologian, faith healer, teacher, and writer, as well as an early feminist. Eventually, she and her students (and some of Quimby's) went on to create the New Thought movement in the form of several liberal theologies and philosophies, including Divine Science, the Unity Church, Religious Science, and so on. It influenced the Meso-Pagan magical systems and religions known as Huna and Wicca (see *Bonewits's Essential Guide to Witchcraft and Wicca* for more on this), as well as the New Age movement of the late 20th and early 21st centuries. Most of the New Thought philosophies are panentheistic, in that deity is seen as transcendent yet present throughout the material universe. Creative energy, or God, is everywhere, and is accessible to humans if they learn to think correctly. New Thought adherents use a lot of affirmations (positive statements spoken or written repeatedly), meditation, prayer, and positive thinking to focus their consciousnesses on health, beauty, love, and prosperity. The New Thought movement also influenced 19th and 20th century Hermetic Philosophy, such as is found in *The Kybalion*.

In 1882, the Society for Psychical Research was founded in England to investigate the many uncanny effects that Spiritualist mediums and independent clairvoyants (literally, clear seers) were producing in séances and stage performances. These researchers, who would eventually become known as parapsychologists, tended to focus their attention on psychic energies as being natural forces of the universe, with no necessary association with spirits. They also tried to differentiate their use of the term "psychic" from the way mainstream science used it (as meaning anything associated with the mind). Eventually they gave up and called themselves parapsychologists—scientists who were going beyond (*para-*) regular psychology in their research. The energies they studied, which they abbreviated as *psi* (from the Greek letter that began the word "psychic"), were originally considered to manifest themselves in one of three ways: through extra-sensory perception (ESP), psychokinesis (PK, or mind over matter), and precognition (knowing the future). In 1971, Isaac suggested that precognition was a subset of a larger category, hypercognition, and that a fourth category of anti-psi was needed to describe to describe psychic phenomena that primarily affected other psychic phenomena. (See Chapter 7, and Isaac's book *Real Magic*, for more on this topic.)

Wilhelm Reich (1897–1957), an early psychiatrist who studied with Sigmund Freud, discovered in the 1930s a type of energy he called *orgone*. He eventually built devices for collecting, concentrating, and generating this energy. Similar to Reichenbach, he believed this energy to be present in all living matter. Unlike Reichenbach, however, he also believed that there was a direct connection between sexual activities and attitudes on the one hand, and the generation or suppression of orgone energy on the other. It's possible that Reichenbach may have believed this as well, but unfortunately he was unable to discuss this publicly during his lifetime. Isaac finds plenty of suggestion in Reichenbach's research (which initially focused on women and children in mental institutions) to indicate that he believed that sexuality played a strong role in why the patients were there in the first place, and why they seemed to have so much extra energy available to be measured.

So perhaps it's not surprising that Reich first discovered orgone energy while doing experiments to measure the bioelectric characteristics of the male orgasm. He combined these experiments with his psychoanalytic training, eventually coming up with the idea of body armoring—that is, physiological damage, including muscle and nerve blocks, caused by repressed sexuality, and leading to a reduced flow of orgone energy throughout the body.

Interestingly, body armoring is a diagnosis still used today by a variety of massage therapists and New Age body workers). Perhaps not surprisingly, Reich advocated frequent orgasms as one treatment method. Unfortunately, when these ideas were seen in the context of his atheism and Marxism, he became a very controversial figure—even among the German Communists, who kicked him out of the Party for writing *The Sexual Revolution*, and for implying that their own puritanism (rooted in the Christian dualism that had influenced Marx) was neurotic. A few years later, he published *The Mass Psychology of Fascism*, in which he pointed out the <u>connections between conservative political movements and sexual repression</u> (a theory that remains valid even today). The Nazis banned the book and drove him out of Germany.

Reich spent many years performing experiments on everything from bacteria and mice to cloud formations and humans, eventually deciding that orgone was a cosmically distributed energy that was "negatively entropic" (creating rather than destroying order). During this time he also claimed that orgone energy could be used to heal both psychological and physical diseases. The latter claim, when combined with his controversial and scandalous ideas and lifestyle, the enemies he had made on both ends of the political spectrum, and his unwillingness to cooperate with a Food and Drug Administration investigation into his "quackery," resulted in the confiscation and burning of his books and papers, and his eventual death in a federal penitentiary. To this day, he is one of the only Americans ever to have his books—and there were many of them, including *The Function of the Orgasm, The Murder of Christ, Listen Little Man!*, and *The Orgone Energy Accumulator, Its Scientific and Medical*

Use—legally banned and publicly burned. Fortunately for the world, most of them were republished a decade after his death.

Reich always conceived of orgone as a 100 percent natural phenomenon (unlike od or vril), with nothing psychical or mystical about it. In his linking it to sexuality, however, Reich perhaps stumbled over something magicians and mystics around the world have known for millennia—namely, that sexual repression and/or expression can have far-reaching effects on people and their environments, and not always through scientifically explainable ways.

Mid- to late-20th century esoteric and metaphysical energy vocabulary tended to mine the growing field of electromagnetic phenomena and technology for its metaphors (though there were plenty of people still using the older terms). For example, in the early and middle decades, telepathy was thought of as a type of "psychic radio," whereas later in the century, such topics as information theory and cybernetics, psychedelic experimentation, quantum physics, chaos theory, as well as more controversial scientific theories such as "morphic resonance" (the idea that energy fields can shape living and nonliving matter), informed the parlance of people now known as New Agers, Neo-Pagans, chaos magicians, and energy workers.

Earlier we mentioned the Theosophical construct of multiple planes or spheres of matter existing at differing vibration rates. *The Kybalion*, an early 20th century book that was very influential among Western magicians, mystics, and psychics, phrased its own esoteric concept of vibrations as follows:

It is a fact well known to modern science, as well as to the Hermetists who have embodied the truth in their "Third Hermetic Principle," that "everything is in motion; everything vibrates; nothing is at rest." From the highest manifestation, to the lowest, everything and all things Vibrate. Not only do they vibrate at different rates of motion, but as in different directions and in a different manner. The degrees of the "rate" of vibrations constitute the degrees of measurement on the Scale of Vibrations— in other words the degrees of the Fourth Dimension. And these degrees form what occultists call "Planes." The higher the degree of rate of vibration, the higher the plane, and the higher the manifestation of Life occupying that plane. So that while a plane is not "a place," nor yet "a state or condition," yet it possesses qualities common to both.

This Principle embodies the truth that 'everything is in motion;' 'everything vibrates;' 'nothing is at rest;' facts which Modern Science endorses, and which each new scientific discovery tends to verify. And yet this Hermetic Principle was enunciated thousands of years ago, by the Masters of Ancient Egypt.[8] This Principle explains that the differences between different manifestations of Matter, Energy, Mind, and even Spirit, result largely from varying rates of Vibration. From THE ALL, which is Pure Spirit, down to the grossest form of Matter, all is in vibration—the higher the vibration, the higher the position in the scale. The vibration of Spirit is at such an infinite rate of intensity and rapidity that it is practically at rest—just as a rapidly moving wheel seems to be motionless. And at the other end of the scale, there are gross forms of matter whose vibrations are so low as to seem at rest. Between these poles, there are millions upon millions of varying degrees of vibration. From corpuscle and electron, atom and molecule, to worlds and universes, everything is in vibratory motion. This is also true on the planes of energy and force (which are but varying degrees of vibration); and also on the mental planes (whose states depend upon vibrations); and even on to the spiritual planes. An understanding of this Principle, with the appropriate formulas, enables Hermetic students to control their own mental vibrations as well as those of others. The Masters also apply this Principle to the conquering of Natural phenomena, in various ways. "He who understands the Principle of Vibration, has grasped the sceptre of power," says one of the old writers.[9]

There are aspects of the electromagnetic spectrum, such as infrared and ultraviolet radiation, that humans can't see directly because their frequencies are shorter or longer then the limits of visible light. Early theorists such as Blavatsky and *The Kybalion*'s authors (The Three Initiates) suggested that anything vibrating too quickly to be seen might disappear altogether from normal perceptions. This theory was based in part on some confusion regarding the related concepts of frequency and vibration. Electromagnetic frequency, as we have already seen, relates to the number of waves in a moving EM flow per unit of distance. Likewise, acoustic frequency consists of the number of waves in moving air per unit of time; thus, sounds we define as higher have a higher frequency. Vibration, however, usually refers to oscillations (back and forth movements) of physical objects, such as a motor or the string on a musical instrument. These vibrations may cause sound frequencies, but they can't be said to exist *as* frequencies. A vibrating violin string may oscillate too quickly for the human eye to track, but it doesn't really ever become invisible to the camera's eye.

Everything vibrates. Some things vibrate quickly, such as the gases we call air (you might remember this from chemistry class). Molecules and atoms vibrate. If molecules vibrate very slowly, you have something solid such as a table or a wall. You can pass your hand through the quick vibrators (think of waving your hand through the air), while the slow vibrators will create more of an impasse (think of banging your head against a brick wall).

But what about the more mystical "vibes"? During the years of the drug culture (the late 1960s to mid-70s), many users of psychedelics noticed objects vibrating and emanating waves of energy. Some noticed their own bodies vibrating and saw energy fields around their hands and feet. Some noticed their vibes and energies changing along with their moods. Some even saw little green men.

For our purposes, it doesn't matter whether these experiences were real in some absolute sense or not. According to the magical laws of infinite and personal universes, such judgments are impossible for mystics and magicians to make. What is important here is that such observations, accurate or not, gave birth to the modern metaphor of inanimate objects and living things having vibrations and emanating energies. The hippies who were a part of the then-emerging New Age movement took it for granted that by modifying their vibes, they could modify their mystical and mundane energies. Because the ways in which they modified their vibes altered their biochemical processes and mental states, they wound up inadvertently duplicating some of what mystics and magicians had been doing for centuries.

In physics, resonance is the tendency of a system to oscillate (vibrate back and forth) with greater strength when excited by energy at a certain frequency; this frequency is known as the system's natural frequency of vibration, or resonant frequency.

For example, if you play a loud G note on a musical instrument near a properly tuned violin, the violin's G-string will respond by vibrating at the same pitch. Mystics and other energy workers tend to think of resonance in a much looser sense, as in the concept of "getting people on the same wavelength" (in the same mood, focused on the same goal). This assumes that the energies being generated by or transmitted through people can coordinate with one another and thus create a stronger effect.

Resonance is often confused with entrainment, which occurs when two oscillating systems affect each other so that they slow down and/or speed up until they are vibrating at the same speed. A classic example of this—one used in religious, magical, mystical, and artistic rituals around the world—is the fact that human heartbeats will entrain themselves to a drumbeat. The sound waves from the drum impinge on the ears and bodies of the people, causing a small if steady vibration in their chest cavities and eardrums. How much of the entrainment in this example is physiological and how much is psychological is difficult to say— we just know it works!

What the Mystical Terms Have in Common

Most of the terms for different kinds of mystical energy seem to refer more or less to the same concept—namely, a postulated energy that is both a life force and a cosmic force. Under this category would fall qi, prana, od, vril, orgone, and mana, all of which are the fundamental terms in their respective systems of metaphysics. (We could probably add the Force from *Star Wars* to this list as well.) Thinking of spirits as localized or distributed packets of energy composed of this life or cosmic force, and which use this force to interact with humans and the mundane, physical world, probably covers the majority of the energies used by mystics, magicians, and healers. Perhaps the other forms of energy, such as ectoplasm, psi, and the Greek Elements, are subcategories of this force, or results of its interactions with energies that are understood as mundane. Physicists will insist, of course, that if any of these energies are real, they must have a quantum (fundamental unit) that exists in fields and can be measured. Perhaps Reich's experiments with his bions and orgone fields were a step in that direction.

We will use all of these terms at various points throughout this book, as we attempt to differentiate the various types of energies. When we want to refer to these energies without making distinctions, we'll simply call them mystical energies. If, how, and where the mystical energies intersect with mundane physical energies will be discussed throughout this book as well. The bottom line, however, is that most if not all of these metaphors and technical terms (including perhaps the ones used by physicists) refer as much to states of consciousness in the participants and observers as they do to any kind of physical or metaphysical existence in an absolute reality, of either a universe or a multiverse.

Perhaps by the end of this book we will come to the conclusion that our ancestors weren't ignorant fools after all, but merely the victims of insufficiently sophisticated measuring devices.

Or not.

A Note on Noticing Mystical Energies

Throughout the book, we will be assuming that you, too, can in some way feel or sense the energies we're discussing. That's not the easiest thing for everyone to do. You may have to train yourself to notice very subtle sensations. Mystical energy can sometimes feel so tenuous, so vague and weak, that it can be easy to dismiss as imagination alone.

At times, you may find yourself saying, "I'm not feeling anything, not really; I'm just telling myself I feel it because I'm supposed to feel something." This is self-sabotage. It may be true on some abstract level of reality, but it's not a useful belief for a magician, psychic, mystic, or other energy worker. For now, honor what you feel, however slight. With practice, you will become more sensitive to these subtle energies and their variations. You may start off with the belief that you won't be able to feel anything, but one day you might realize that you sense subtle energies so strongly and so often that your real problem has become insufficient psychic shielding.

Chapter 2

Magic and Its Laws

Do You Believe in Magic?

Because much of what we'll be discussing in the rest of the book involves magical and psychic ideas and activities, let's define these terms clearly to begin with, so that you will know what we have in mind when we use such terms. Here is how we will be using the word "magic" in this book, phrased in three different ways:

✦ A general term for arts, sciences, philosophies, and technologies concerned with (a) understanding and using the various altered states of consciousness that make it possible to have access to and control over one's psychic talents; and (b) the uses and abuses of those psychic talents to change interior and/or exterior realities.

✦ A science and an art comprised of a system of concepts and methods that heighten human emotions, alter the electrochemical balance of the metabolism, and use associational techniques and devices to concentrate and focus this emotional energy, thus modulating the energies broadcasted by the human body—usually to affect other energy patterns, whether animate or inanimate, but occasionally to affect the personal energy pattern.

✦ A collection of rule-of-thumb techniques designed to get one's psychic talents to do more or less what one wants. (More often than not, one hopes!)[1]

Sharp-eyed readers will have noticed that the second definition of magic says something about "emotional energies" and "energies broadcasted by the human body." We hope that what we mean by those phrases will be a great deal clearer by the time the reader has finished this book. All three definitions imply the existence of something called "psychic talents," so let's take a look at what "psychic" means.

The word comes from the Greek *psukhikos*, meaning "of the mind or soul," and from the root *psukhe*, meaning "breath," "life," and "soul." According to the *Shorter Oxford English Dictionary* (*SOED*), the modern English word "psyche" is used mostly to refer to a psychological and/or spiritual entity, as in one's "psyche," or the words "psychology" and "psychotherapy." As Isaac put it in *Rites of Worship*:

The *SOED* tells us that "psychic" [as a noun] means "a person who is regarded as particularly susceptible to supernatural or paranormal influence; a medium, a clairvoyant," as well as "the realm or sphere of psychical phenomena." As an adjective, "psychic" or "psychical" denotes the characteristics of such persons or phenomena. The latter version of the word is defined separately by the *SOED* as "of, pertaining to, or concerned with phenomena or faculties which appear to transcend the laws of physics and are attributed by some to spiritual or hyperphysical agency; involving paranormal phenomena of the mind, parapsychological." The "-al" ending has become rather quaint and is rarely used today.

In Christian theology [according to the SOED], "psychic" was used to mean "pertaining to the natural or animal soul [the subconscious], as distinct from the spirit." This usage, rooted in the ancient belief that people had more than one soul/spirit, was the sense in which the Theosophists, Spiritualists, and other occultists of the nineteenth century used it. The attitude that psychic things were inferior in virtue and value to spiritual things remains in [Theosophical and Rosicrucian] literature, and that of many modern [occult and metaphysical] groups who are descended from them.

Webster's defines "psychic" as "of, arising in, or relating to the psyche," and "not physical or organic; lying outside the sphere of physical science or knowledge; governed by, concerned with, or acting on the psyche or self." When referring to a person, Webster's says it means someone who is "sensitive to nonphysical forces and influences, marked by extraordinary or mysterious sensitivity, perception, or understanding."

That brings us much closer to the way modern occultists, magicians, and parapsychologists use the term, to refer to rare or seldom-used powers of the mind, which are capable of causing effects that appear to contradict the mainstream worldview of western science and philosophy...

Modern psychologists, by the way, still use the word "psychic" to refer to all sorts of mental activities, including the perception and/or manifestation of Jungian archetypes of the collective unconscious.

The term psychic talent is used to refer to abilities such as telepathy, clairvoyance, psychokinesis, precognition, the antipsi powers, and so forth.[2]

A large part of what mystics, magicians, energy workers, and shamanic healers do is rooted in the existence of these psychic powers, which are focused and controlled through traditional methods often termed "magic." This book won't make the argument for the reality of these powers and talents, as most readers will already know from their personal experience that these things are real enough to make their lives interesting—sometimes far more interesting than they really want!

Thaumaturgy and Theurgy—Targets and Goals

The word *thaumaturgy* comes from the Greek *thaumaturgia*, or "wonder-working" (note the *–urgia*, or "work/energy," suffix). Originally, any "miracle" worker was called a thaumaturgist, whether he or she was a holy person, a magician, or a prestidigitator (stage magician). As we use the word, thaumaturgy is magic that is done for mundane or secular purposes, such as making rain come or go, healing the sick, or improving the fertility of crops. Any magical act may be considered thaumaturgical, even if it is done within a religious context, such as invoking a rain deity or doing a Buddhist healing.

The word *theurgy* also comes from the Greek, in this case *theurgia*, or "god-working" (or "working with divine energy").[3] A theurgist was a person who was using magic and ritual in an effort to contact deities or other benevolent spirits, and to attain mystical knowledge. Most of the ancient gnostics[4] ("knowers"), members of what may have been the first New Age movement, were theurgists. We use theurgy to refer to magic done for religious and/or psychotherapeutic purposes; in order to attain salvation, empowerment, or personal growth; and/or to strengthen the Goddesses and Gods, and/or to simply experience a sense of oneness with a chosen deity or the cosmos as a whole.

There is a very strong bias in both Western and Eastern mystical literature in favor of theurgy and against thaumaturgy. (Of course, the Eastern occultists use different words.) However, the fact is that these two words simply indicate opposite ends of a continuous range of activity and intent. Locating where a proposed use of mystical energy belongs on that continuum is an important part of energy workings of all varieties.[5]

Now let's take a look at an important distinction to be made in all forms of magic (though it is seldom made clear)—namely, the difference between the target and the goal of one's efforts. Let's say you are an energy healer who is presented with a case of lung cancer. Do you pump lots of generic healing and growth energy into the person's body in general or into their lungs? Why or why not? If they are at a distance from you, do you visualize them as sick or as well? Most experienced healers know that different types of energy can produce different effects. For example, you might send "red" energy to "burn up" the cancer cells in the client's lungs, then follow up with "green" energy to promote rapid growth of healthy tissue in the lungs and throughout the body. Whatever your choice of metaphors, you would visualize the client as healthy and whole, not as sick and diseased. If you just pump growth energy into him or her, you might easily make the cancer worse; if you visualize him or her as sick, your energies might just reinforce that energy state instead

target vs. goal

of promoting healing. Understanding how to make such practical decisions is a matter of distinguishing clearly between the targets and goals of your workings. The targets are specific objects or energy patterns you need to change in order to manifest a specific goal or goals. In our example, tumors would be targets, while a healthy body would be the goal.

Multisensory Focusing Methods

Traditional mystics and magicians sometimes use wands, crystals, or other objects as "lenses" to focus the flow of their mystical energies. However, this focus is usually thought of in terms of the mental focus of the energy worker(s) and the clients or patients involved. To aid in attaining this focus, various rituals are performed. So what is a ritual? Let's see how it is defined in *Rites of Worship*:

A "ritual" or "rite" is any ordered sequence of events, actions, and/or directed thoughts, especially one that is meant to be repeated in the same (however loosely or tightly defined) manner each time, that is designed to produce a predictable altered state of consciousness (ASC) within which certain results may be obtained.[6]

The results may be mundane, as in achieving efficiency at your job through the ingestion of coffee in order to alter your state of consciousness to "awake," and thus to facilitate the accomplishment of your morning tasks.

The desired results may instead be intellectual ones, as with the discoveries made through the various rituals known as "the scientific method." Or they might be artistic, as in the ritual called "Beethoven's Ninth Symphony." They might be psychological, as in the repetitive behavior of people suffering from Obsessive

Compulsive Disorder. But for the purposes of this book, we'll restrict the use of the word "ritual" to refer to those that are designed to produce various magical, psychic, and/or spiritual results.

Every ritual, whether artistic, scientific, magical, or religious, (and whether perceived by its performers as a ritual or not) is an ordered sequence of events designed to produce a particular result. The particular activities or techniques employed in the ritual, as well as the sequence as a whole (the ritual itself), produce altered states of consciousness (ASCs). Well-executed ritual contains a sequence of managed ASCs appropriate both to their place in the sequence and to the overall goal at hand. The activities and techniques—smudging, centering, circumambulation, vocalization, movement, and so on—are ordered in such a way as to increasingly focus our attention to the work at hand. In other words, the activities remove us from everyday consciousness to an ASC that will allow us to work the magic. A good ritual will reach its peak or peaks of focus and intensity, and then return us incrementally to normal, everyday consciousness.

Therefore, selecting the appropriate activities, techniques, and rituals to be used in any situation hinges upon understanding what ASCs, and in what order, are most likely to achieve the stated goal or result. This is not to say that the average crystal healer, Reiki master, or Buddhist priest is consciously aware of what she or he is doing. Despite superficial differences in their vocabularies, all of the disparate traditions of energy working are doing pretty much the same thing.

Although we hope that all of this is very obvious to you, we have often found that it is real news indeed to lots of folks in the New Age, mystical, magical, and Neo-Pagan communities.

So many people confuse "perceived energy" with "effective energy," and "state change" with "appropriate state change." The choice of what sights, sounds, and smells to use in your rituals depends in part on precisely what ASCs you are looking to create, and in part on what goals you wish to achieve. Fortunately, the task of making these choices wisely is made easier by the laws of magic.

Laws? Of Magic?

The laws of magic are rule-of-thumb observations that magicians, mystics, folklorists, and anthropologists have made over the course of many centuries to describe how they think magic works. Depending on who is counting, there are anywhere from two to more than 20 of them. Different people use different names for these laws, but the ones we will use in this book are the ones Isaac made famous in 1971, when he published the first edition of *Real Magic*, with some minor additions that have occurred to him over the years.

Because the different laws interact with each other in complex ways, we find it useful to visualize them as a set of overlapping circles, as shown on the accompanying illustrations. Sometimes the overlap areas are important enough to become laws in themselves, as shown by the heavier lines around the laws of finite senses, true falsehoods, positive and negative attraction, and names. Let's begin with an overview chart, Figure 7 shown on page 69.

As you can see, some of the laws are represented by big circles—including the biggest one for the law of unity—and some by small. This is to illustrate that some of the laws are more important, or at least more inclusive, than others. Some of the laws, such as contagion and similarity, are entirely contained

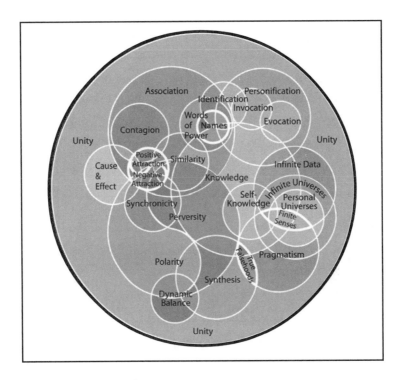

Figure 7: *All of the laws of magic.*

within these larger circles, indicating that they are sublaws of a larger law (in this case, the law of association). All of the laws and sublaws overlap at least one other law, while some of them, such as true falsehoods or finite senses, exist mostly in the overlap between two others.

Let's go around the chart clockwise, beginning with the upper right or northeast quarter shown in Figure 8 on page 70. This will include the laws of unity, personification, identification, invocation, evocation, knowledge, self-knowledge, infinite data, infinite universes, and personal universes.

The law of unity is known in philosophy as *monism*, the concept that "all is one." This statement may seem obvious (that is, if something wasn't part of the totality of all existence, how

Law of Unity

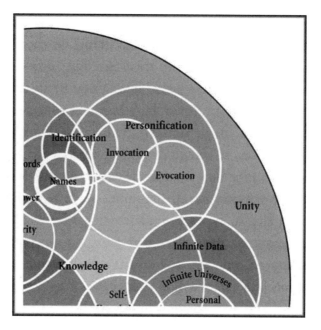

Figure 8: *The laws of magic, upper right quadrant.*

would we know it was there?); however, for mystics and magicians, as well as for physicists, the idea that everything is connected to everything else is an important and fundamental assumption. This idea could be referring to the postulated quantum structure of the multiverse (the totality of all possible universes) that underlies everything we can perceive directly or indirectly. Or it could be referring to the fact that a clever magician or energy worker can always figure out a way to connect ideas, people, objects, and/or energy patterns as needed in order to achieve her or his objectives. Or it could be another way of referring to a cosmically distributed energy or spirit that an energy worker, mystic, or magician can tap into to achieve his or her goals.

The law of personification states that any thing, place, or concept can be thought of as having human characteristics, and

Law of
Personification

that this is frequently very useful. This law is all about the many ways that people in general tend to attribute personhood, or at least personality and volition, to objects and abstract ideas. When you assume that a cosmically distributed energy field is a Supreme Being (with personality, thoughts, desires, emotions, and so on) with which you can interact, you are personifying it. When you see a volcano or a thunderstorm as a deity, or nature as Mother Nature, or your native land as Uncle Sam, John Bull, or Érin, you are personifying those things. When you appeal to Justice, Freedom, Truth, Fertility, or Prosperity as the "spirits" of these abstract concepts, you are personifying them, too. These common mental processes are often seen by anthropologists and more moderate religious scholars as the origins of the deities and spirits common to most if not all cultures.

The law of identification states that if you spend enough time meditating upon a spirit or concept, and correlating different aspects of yourself with different aspects of it, you can psychologically merge with it. Christian and Buddhist mystics have been doing this for centuries, leading to numerous reported mystical visions and paranormal events. From an energy worker's perspective, this law is talking about getting yourself on the same wavelength as the entity you wish to emulate, perhaps achieving morphic resonance.

The laws of invocation and evocation may or may not be different names for the same sublaw of personification. How you see this will depend upon on your point of view about the location of the spirit or entity with whom you are communicating. If you feel that the entity is outside of you, and you are pulling its energy into yourself, that's *invocation*; conversely, if you think the entity is inside of you, and you are pulling its energy out of yourself and into someone, something, or someplace else, that's

evocation. Another option is that you may wish to have a conversation with a spirit or entity that is inside of you, in which
case you will *invoke* it—or, you may prefer to converse with it
in a nice safe magical triangle (holding cell) by *evoking* it there.
Essentially, both of these laws state that all of these communication processes are possible, and often useful. Certainly, personification is a universal human habit, whether you are
personifying a Supreme Being as a grouchy Middle Eastern
patriarch, or you are yelling at a chunk of sidewalk you just
tripped over as if it had ears.

Personification, invocation, evocation, and identification are
all involved in the ancient magical and mystical theories of how
the human microcosm ("little universe") is similar to the macrocosm ("big universe"). Thus, ancient astrologers assigned different
zodiac signs to rule different parts of the human body, from Aries
in the head to Pisces in the feet, and Hebrew Cabalists matched
different parts of the human body with various "spheres of emanation" from God on the "Tree of Life." Whether such theories
were rooted in the idea of lower pitches of energy vibration
matching certain higher ones as mathematical functions is unknown (although it doesn't stop people from saying so).

The law of knowledge is very simple: knowledge is power.
The more you know about something or someone, the easier it
is to coordinate your energy with them or "get on the same wavelength." And the law of self-knowledge is its most important
sublaw: know thyself! The more you know about your own
strengths, weaknesses, skills, needs, and habits, the more successful your energy work will be, whether mystical, magical, or
mundane. This is because the energy worker's own body, mind,
and soul are her or his most important "tools."

Law of Infinite Data

At first glance, the law of infinite data seems to be merely a philosophical comment about the infinite number of things that can be learned, whether you think of data as facts, opinions, observations, theories, or something else. It's a practical law in that it encourages mystics and magicians to forever continue learning; however, it also leads inevitably to the law of infinite universes, which states that there are an infinite number of ways in which an infinite amount of data can be structured or perceived. The fact that every person organizes the data he or she perceives into his or her own universe leads to the law of personal universes—namely, that everyone lives in their own private cosmos. Now if, as some physicists have philosophized, consciousness is a natural property of the physical universe(s), and if every particle has its own consciousness (however you define it), it's possible that the laws of infinite and personal universes are identical, or paradoxically, even subsets of each other—but now we're now talking in metaphors only loosely based on physics, and mundane logic may not apply. From an energy working perspective, these laws suggest that anything and everything is possible (though some things are more probable than others), which can lead to a great deal of self-confidence and out-of-the-box creative approaches.

In the lower right or southeast quarter of our chart, Figure 9 shown on page 74, we have the laws of finite senses, pragmatism, true falsehoods, and synthesis.

finite senses

The law of finite senses is based on another simple observation: finite beings have finite perceptions. While parts of us may be connected to (or might actually be) infinite resources, in our day-to-day lives we all have our sensory limitations. Most human beings cannot see the ultraviolet or infrared frequencies on the EM spectrum, for example. This doesn't mean there aren't

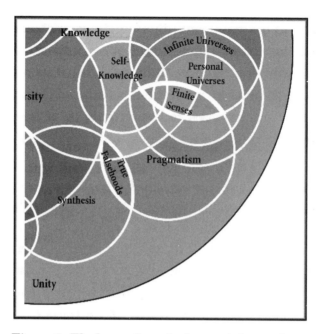

Figure 9: *The laws of magic, lower right quadrant.*

colors or other interesting bits of information to be gathered from those parts of the spectrum—we just can't see them without special equipment designed to surmount our sensory limitations. As mentioned earlier, we can't see on the microscopic *or* the macroscopic levels, which is why we invented microscopes and telescopes. And there's always that dark matter and dark energy (see chapter 4) that our unaided senses may never be able to perceive.

These limitations probably also exist on the psychic, magical, spiritual, and even physical levels of perception, which is why a certain amount of humility is a good habit for energy workers of all varieties to get into—especially those who refuse to acknowledge any limits at all. If information that we can't sense or comprehend exists, then we have no way of knowing how much of it there is, so such information might as well be infinite, which, of course, ties this law in with the preceding ones.

The law of pragmatism is familiar to engineers, politicians, and single parents: if something works, it's true—no matter what level or area of reality you happen to be focused on. This law encourages energy workers of all varieties to stick with methods that produce desired results, regardless of whether those methods make sense to hostile observers. Frankly (or Gothically), there are very few energy workers, whether they call themselves magicians, mystics, psychics, healers, or shamans, who do a lot of digging into how and why what they do works, as long as it works more often than not. As one mundane example, generations of European herbalists gave willow bark tea to clients with headaches, without knowing anything about the pharmacology of aspirin. As you can see from the chart, the law of pragmatism doesn't have an obvious connection to the law of personification;[7] however, the former would clearly support the latter, because treating aspects of the universe as if they were people is sometimes effective.

The law of true falsehoods follows from this, in that a myth or superstition on one level of reality may be a handy concept or tool on another. In other words, the fact that something is a paradox doesn't mean it's not true. This is an area in which Western dualism seriously impedes subtle and creative analysis of complex issues. If you live in a personal universe in which every single statement must be judged as 100 percent true or 100 percent false—white or black, right or wrong, good or evil—then paradoxes, contradictions, and other complications will be seen as deeply threatening on both philosophical and emotional levels. Thus, any variation in a received truth will be seen as a slippery slope to the opposite extreme of absolute falseness. Fortunately we aren't dualists, so we're free to perceive and discuss the million-odd colors of the natural world, rather than just the black and the white.

anti-absolutist
- dualist

The law of synthesis is connected to true falsehoods on one side, and the laws of polarity and perversity on the other. It says that if you spend enough time contemplating paradoxes, you will eventually arrive at new truths synthesized from the most useful or pragmatic parts of each contradiction. This law was most famously posited by ancient Greek philosophers as "thesis, antithesis, and synthesis," also called the dialectic or formal argument. Today it is most commonly attributed to Friedrich Hegel (1770–1831), Karl Marx (1818–1883), and their respective followers. The dialectic holds that any idea (especially a complex "-ism") can be stated as a simple thesis, but in order to be fully understood, it must be contrasted with an opposite idea, or antithesis (literally, setting opposite). Sufficient thought, mystical contemplation, or linguistic fiddling will inevitably lead to a new, blended idea—a synthesis—that will be superior in truth value (truer on more levels of reality?) to the original two. Of course, Zen Buddhists have been teaching a very similar idea for over a millennium, though without Hegel's and Marx's insistence on rational analysis.

In the lower left or southwest quarter of our chart shown in Figure 10 on page 77, we have the laws of polarity, perversity, dynamic balance, cause and effect, and sychronicity.

The laws of polarity and perversity form a large yin-yang symbol, and are overlapped by several other laws. The law of polarity is another way of stating the thesis/antithesis concept, only without the dualist baggage of assuming that opposites must be pitted against each other in some hostile fashion. Instead, polarity holds that any concept can be understood as consisting of one or more pairs of opposites, each of which contains the essence of the other within it. Male means nothing without female, up without down, hot without cold, old without new,

one implies
the other

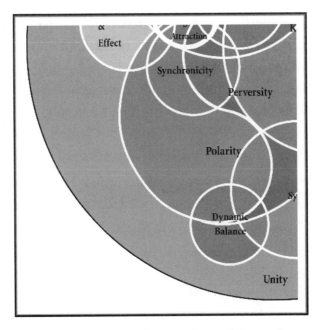

Figure 10: *The laws of magic, lower left quadrant.*

and so on. This way of looking at opposites tends to lead to embraces rather than warfare, with subsequent conceptual offspring rather than corpses.

The law of perversity is not the law that states that people who disagree with accepted truth must be perverts. Rather, this is the law that is better known in the modern West as Murphy's Law—namely, if anything can go wrong it will, and usually in a way that will be the most annoying. This is also known as the law of unintended consequences. The purpose of this magical law is to remind energy workers that if they have any subconscious issues regarding a spell, meditation, artwork, or healing they plan to do, the results may not be exactly as expected. Even if things don't go awry, the results might be surprising!

Because it appears that all psychic, magical, spiritual, artistic, sexual, and other creative energies are filtered through the subconscious hopes, fears, and assumptions of the people involved, it is always wise to pay attention to internal processes. Certainly, there are plenty of people, even highly evolved energy workers, who have self-destructive circuits in their subconscious minds or spirits, so thinking ahead about the various ways your planned work could go astray is a good policy in general. This doesn't mean you can't think positive, but it does mean that you shouldn't go tossing your energies around carelessly.

The law of dynamic balance is another practical law (have you noticed how many of them are?) that urges the necessity of keeping all the different aspects of your being in a state of dynamic, flexible, ever-changing balance, rather than in a static or rigid one. From the chart you can see that it intersects the laws of polarity, perversity, and synthesis—polarity and perversity because the physical, mental, emotional, spiritual, and artistic sides of you are often seen in sets of opposites; and synthesis to remind you to rise above (or dive below, or run around) those polar oppositions to create the syntheses that enable you to stay balanced and avoid extremes.

The law of cause and effect works in the same way with mystical energies as it does with other kinds: certain behaviors, activities, or events, when subjected to certain factors or circumstances, will result in more or less predictable results. Witness the following examples: if you throw a ball into the air, it will usually fall down; if you follow the same sequence of moves in a game, you will usually get the same results afterward; and if you keep hitting your head against a stone wall,[8] you will usually experience a headache. This law works whether it's pool balls, subatomic particles, or galaxies that are colliding with one another, or if organic or chemical fertilizers are being used on crops, or if spells are being cast—just with very different levels of predictability involved.

What does this portend for energy workers? Well, most of the time this is a positive thing. For example, if a high wind arises almost every time you whistle on a boat, then whistling is definitely worth trying if you need some wind in your sails. Sometimes, however, this cause and effect can be a negative thing: if you try to heal someone's menstrual cramps by feeding energy from your hands into her belly, and you get menstrual cramps yourself every time, then it's probably time to try a different approach!

The law of synchronicity, named after Carl Jung's (1875–1961) theory of meaningful coincidences, says simply that two events occurring at about the same time may have a connection other than just the time. In other words, some coincidences are more than "mere." In the religion of Scientism,[9] which is very popular among professional debunkers of psychics, the phrase "it was only a coincidence" is often used as a mantra to avoid thinking about possible connections that might challenge their assumptions and worldviews. Oddly enough, conservative members of certain other religions tend to use the same mantra (alternating with "it was a demonic deception") when observing the successful results of magical, psychic, or spiritual activities done by members of competing faiths.

Is it a coincidence if the lights go on or off in your living room almost every time you clap your hands? Perhaps you have a sound-activated light switch installed, but if you don't, and there isn't a mischievous someone hiding behind the couch and unplugging the lights, then you have to decide how many times you will repeat the event before you decide that something more than coincidence is going on. If you learn over time that doing 15 minutes of yoga stretches before you get on your bicycle to ride to work means that you usually arrive less tired, then pretty soon you'll say the one "caused" the other "effect." It could just be meaningless coincidences at work, but probably not.

Officer Bill of the Physics Police has an interesting story that ties into this topic of coincidence, as well as some of the other concepts mentioned in this chapter:

I was nearing the end of my graduate student research, and writing a paper for publication on the work I'd done. It had been a long and complex analysis, and had taken years longer than most grad-student physics research projects. It was well-known in the physics lab that I was Wiccan, and my thesis advisor and I would occasionally joke about it. One day, as we were working on my paper, I happened to ask, "Do you want me to cast a spell on this so we can finally get it done?"

We chuckled on this for a moment, and he replied, "Sure, why not?"

I said, "You have to focus a spell on exactly what you want. What should the goal of the spell be?"

He thought for a moment and said seriously, "I want what all scientists want: to get the right answer."

That weekend, I discussed the situation with my Wiccan group. We agreed that we'd focus the spell's energies on the minds of [the targets] working on this research problem. The goal would be to produce clarity of thought that would lead us to the right answer. We cast the circle, performed the ritual, and cast the spell. Within the next two weeks, we discovered a substantive flaw in the analysis technique I had used. I had to redo a portion of the work, delaying both my graduation and the publication of the paper by two or three months. Students of magic will note how the initial goal (getting it done quickly) got changed to a different goal (getting the right answer), how we selected the minds of the scientists involved (including myself) as the targets, and how the effects of the spell achieved the goal.

To continue this story, I have to get mildly technical. My research concerned measuring the coupling constant of the strong nuclear force. The value I measured was 0.119 ± 0.005. For those who care, the first number represents a central value, and the second is the margin of error on the measurement.

I graduated and received my Ph.D. in high-energy physics. My paper was published in *Physical Review Letters*. About a year later, a review article was published summarizing all the values of the strong coupling constant from different physics experiments that measure it. (I should explain here that my experiment was only one of many approaches to making this measurement.) The values of all the measurements from the different experiments (including mine) were summed, weighted by their errors, and adjusted for other factors. The final result from summing the results from all the different experiments? It was 0.119 ± 0.005...and there was no particular physics reason why the final world's value should agree with my value, including the margin of error.

That's the end of the anecdote, but there's more to say that concerns the topics that Isaac brings up in this book. The events in [this] story took place in the mid-1990s. Shortly after they occurred, I kept quiet about happened; one of the things I was taught as a witch was to be silent about a spell for as long as you wished the effects to last. After enough time elapsed that my results were no longer relevant to my career or the scientific community in general, I began to tell the story occasionally.

When I tell the story in front of witches, other magical practitioners, or the average [layperson], the usual reaction is a nod, a smile, perhaps a chuckle. Once I told this story where there was another physicist present. Her reaction was, "That was the worst excuse for the existence of magic that I have ever heard."

Somebody got up on the wrong side of the particle accelerator that morning! Apparently the other physicist assumed that "it was only a coincidence" that Bill's results were identical to the one the world's physicists settled on. Perhaps if she had enquired about how many other physicists had gotten precisely that measurement and had (or had not) done spells to assist their research, she might have had a bigger coincidence to swallow. Of course, if she only knew just how many working scientists are also practicing magicians or mystics, and who use their skills to enhance their scientific research, she and many others would be quite shocked.

The law of synchronicity encourages magicians, mystics, spiritualists, healers, and other energy workers to pay attention to sequences of events, even those that don't seem to be connected. Maybe they are, maybe they aren't, or maybe they are some of the time but not always. Time and experience will tell. Perhaps more importantly, we have both noticed amazing incidents of synchronicity during times in our lives when we are happy, healthy, and working with mystical energies on a regular basis. Therefore, we prefer to see the presence of such coincidences as "magical temperature readings" of how balanced we are.

In the upper left or northwest quarter of our chart, shown in Figure 11, we have the laws of association, contagion, similarity, positive attraction, negative attraction, words of power, and names.

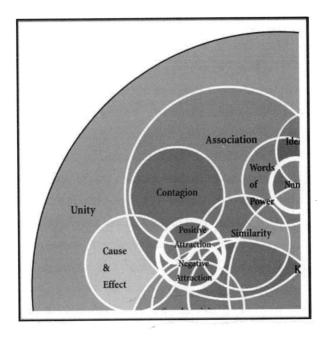

Figure 11: *The laws of magic, upper left quadrant.*

The law of association is the most important of these laws, on par with knowledge and personification, even though it is not as well know as its two major sublaws, contagion and similarity. The law of association states that if two ideas, persons, places, or things have something in common with one another, then they can affect each other through that commonality. For example, let's say you want to do a distant healing on your mother. Her favorite music is the Beatles and her favorite perfume is patchouli (Baby Boomer, we assume). In that case you might want to put *Sgt. Pepper* on the stereo and light up a stick of patchouli incense. Doing these things will assist the healing on two levels: Consciously, they will remind you of her and help you to maintain your focus on the job at hand. Mystically, she has a connection to everyone who grew up with that music and that smell, which means that your energy could skip along those channels to reach her more effectively. Those of you who have done distant healing, whatever your method, probably already know that it would also help to have a lock of your mother's hair or an old hanky of hers, not to mention a photo or realistic drawing of her. These two factors involve the law of contagion and the law of similarity, respectively. The former states that objects in physical connection remain so after separation, while the latter states that things that are similar in appearance, sound, taste, and so on can be used to mystically affect each other. Physical connection and sensory similarity are two of the more simple kinds of association that can exist, but the former could involve quantum entanglement as well.

The law of positive attraction and the law of negative attraction are another yin-yang pair of laws (or sublaws, in this case). The law of positive attraction states that the kind of energy you send out into the multiverse is the kind that returns to you (though it may not always be experienced as positive). This law is better known in magical circles than the law of negative attraction, which warns us that sometimes you get the *opposite* of what you send out—"no good deed goes unpunished," as some would put it. Think of it as an ironic twist on the law of positive attraction. Look at where these two sublaws are placed on the chart: over the cloverleaf intersections of contagion, similarity, cause and effect, and sychronicity, and overlapping both polarity and perversity. Obviously, Murphy is an energy worker!

Meditation on the description of the other laws will help to make it clear that energy can be attracted in both positive and negative ways, and that it is wisest to avoid using "positive" and "negative" as strictly judgmental terms.

The law of words of power states that words can have powerful effects, and some words more than others. You may recognize this as a function of simple psychology or neurolinguistic programming. However, in many mystical and magical traditions, from Hinduism and Buddhism, to Hebrew Cabala and Ceremonial Magic, it is believed that certain words have an additional power based solely on their sounds, especially when properly chanted, sung, or vibrated in the chest. Names, of course, are a subset of words, and the law of names states that if you know the name of something or someone, you will be able to make a direct, magical connection to that thing or person (or deity) more easily. This is especially true, for example, if you know someone's baby name or pet name, because this is connected to his or her inner child—the source of much of a person's psychological and psychic energy. Even better is to know someone's "true" name—that is, their metaphysically and spiritually true name, such as the one given to someone at birth by a shaman or medicine person—because this name will be a precise representation of their spiritual essence.

If you check back to the complete chart of the laws, you will notice that these two laws overlap the laws of knowledge, personification, and identification. This illustrates the fact that using the right words to talk to the correctly named person is often crucial to a successful energy working. If you are invoking the assistance of a deity or ancestor, for example, knowing their name and how to pronounce it correctly could help you to get their spiritual attention. Mystics, magicians, clergy, and other energy workers have long believed in the importance of having clear vocabulary—which is why we spend so much time in this book defining things!

Modern Physics and the Laws of Magic

Officer Bill of the Physics Police writes:

When Isaac told me he planned a section with this title, I was reminded of an old joke: "I have a chapter in my thesis called 'Sex and the Single Physics Graduate Student.' It consists of one sentence: 'The two things have nothing to do with each other.'" However, that joke (you laughed, right?) may be too facile an answer. Elsewhere I stated that as a physicist and witch, I have a foot in two worlds, and that I keep them separate. But one of my first teachers in the Craft was Isaac, and I can hear him say, "There is a connection between those worlds, and that connection is you. You just said so." I'm not vain enough to think that Isaac is going to devote a section of his book to discussing me (actually, he's already given me a portion of a chapter in another of his books).[10] Rather, I'd generalize the statement to say that the connections between modern physics and the laws of magic are people: anyone who's heard any of the principles of physics who then applies them magically.

Isaac has pointed out in the past that, to a large extent, science has supplied the new mythos of the modern era. Instead of angels and demons and fairies, we have UFOs and alien invasions. A physicist might say that the principles of quantum mechanics have nothing to do with the laws of magic; a mythologist would delight in how a healer would make use of the idea of quantum entanglement to visualize a spell working on a cancer patient on the other side of the planet.

As a matter of fact, I (Isaac) have a distance healing technique that might actually be making use of the quantum entanglement idea. This technique involves making a magical link between the center of a circle in the healer's presence, and the center of another circle made around the patient. I always thought it was based on the concept of the sacred center (discussed by Mircea Eliade in his writings about comparative mythology and religion)—namely, that all sacred centers everywhere are the same place spiritually. The center of a circle is an infinitely small point, much like a subatomic particle. Perhaps the pouring of mystical energies into the center of one circle alters that center, thus making a comparable alteration in a distant circle, from which the energies pour out to affect the target person.[11]

To this, Officer York adds:

Physics has nothing much to say about many or even most of the laws; they're more principles of the human mind than of the physical world. Since magic is founded in psychic talents, which in turn represent the interplay of the physical world with some portion of the human mind or spirit, it is not surprising to find a human stamp on the magical laws.

The Law of Unity does find an echo in physicists' quest for a "Theory of Everything," a single physical theory that would account for all physical phenomena, without exception. Ironically, this remains a Holy Grail rather than an achieved goal for physicists. The two great success stories of twentieth-century physics, quantum mechanics and general relativity, do appear between them to explain all the known forces, particles, and interactions. However, they don't qualify as even two pieces of a Theory of Everything, because they're incompatible and irreconcilable.

Unity, and the lesser law of contagion, also bring to mind the phenomenon of quantum entanglement. Any particles—by extension, any two objects whatsoever—that have interacted in the past, are entangled. Most of the time this entanglement has no observable effects. At least, that's what we think now. But in addition to being a theoretical prediction, entanglement is also an experimentally proven fact, observed in increasingly sophisticated lab setups since the 1970s. Entanglement has been confirmed to be a part of the real physical universe we live in. The proofs that most forms of entanglement are unobservable, on the other hand, are part of the theory of quantum mechanics—a theory that could be replaced by a better theory overnight, if we found another theory that accounted for everything that QM does and a few more things besides.

It's possible that *string theory*—the idea that absolutely everything, from subatomic particles to colliding galactic clusters, consists of infinitesimally small strings or loops of vibrating energy—might provide that longed-for Theory of Everything (not to mention vindicating generations of Theosophists who have insisted that everything is vibrations). Interested readers may enjoy a book titled *The Science Of The Craft: Modern Realities in the Ancient Art of Witchcraft*, by William H. Keith Jr. The author discusses how various ideas of modern physics are eerily similar to many of the laws of magic, then goes on to suggest his own "laws of quantum magic."

Assumptions for the Rest of the Book

For the rest of this book, we are going to assume that magic is at least as real as sculpture or poetry or music, and that physical aspects of the universe(s) surrounding magicians and mystics, similar to those surrounding artists and musicians, have reciprocal relationships with the mystical and creative energies being used by these and other energy workers. Just what those relationships are—or might be someday—will be the focus of our discussions. For now, we will ask the reader's indulgence in a beginner's warm-up exercise that deliberately makes no clear distinction between mystical energies and energies that might be considered physical or psychological.

Exercise 1:

The Pre-exercise Exercise

Being aware of your own energies—where they are, what's happening in your body—is critical to solitary energy work, and even more so when working with others. Being aware of the energies around you can be critical to understanding how you learn.

We'll begin with what we can call the ambient energy—the energy that surrounds you at any given time. You must deal with ambient energy any time you need to do anything at all, because the ways in which your surroundings affect you will affect how difficult or easy it is for you to do an exercise. Practice noticing ambient energy in different situations and what effect it has on you. How? It's as easy as stop, look, listen, and remember.

Step 1

Pause what you're doing, anywhere, anytime. (Okay, maybe not while driving. Pull over first.) Take a look around yourself. What is in your field of vision—what do you see? You might be inside or outside. You might be in an urban, suburban, or rural area. You might be looking at a parking lot, a field of flowers, the inside of a subway car, or your own living room. You may be under open sky, or under a roof, or under an umbrella. It may be bright sunlight, candlelight, or as dark as can be.

Is there a lot of space around you? Notice how far you can see—are there walls (or rocks or trees) a few feet in front of you, or can you see for miles? Is your field of vision filled with many objects, as in a cluttered room, on a city street, or in a dense forest? Or is it empty, like a bare hallway or an expanse of ocean? Are there many bright colors, a few colorful spots, or is everything monochromatic?

Notice how many other people are around. Are they close to you or far away? Are they all in one group, in many groups, or alone? Are they standing still or moving around? Are they all moving together (as in a dance), moving in the same direction (as in boarding a bus), or heading every which way (as in a mall)? How do you fit in? Are you part of a group? Are you moving like the other people move, or sitting or standing apart?

Take inventory of the noise level. Do you hear one voice, many voices, or no voices? Do you hear the wind, crickets, or automobiles? Is there music playing, the roar of the surf, or the banging and booming of a construction site? Is it so quiet you can hear yourself breathe? Or do your ears hurt?

Notice all this input from the environment.

Step 2

Now, notice yourself. Notice your body. Are your muscles tight or loose? Are you feeling any pain? Is your clothing comfortable? Are you warm, cold, or just right? How about your breathing? Is it deep and slow, or shallow and light? Is your heart beating slowly or quickly? Is it difficult to sit still, or do you feel very relaxed? Are you ready to go, or are you tapped out?

Notice your feelings. Do you feel upbeat or grumpy? Is it difficult to pay attention to what you are doing, or are you able to concentrate easily? Are you glad the other people are there? Or do you wish they would go away? Do you like what you are seeing and what you are hearing?

Step 3

Now for the most important part: Remember what was going on around you when you were feeling what you were feeling. Remember what your body felt like when you were feeling good, mellow, or edgy. Remember what was going on around you when you were able to concentrate easily or when you were easily distracted. Remember when the energy around you felt as though it was helping you in what you were trying to do just then, and when it got in the way. Note how tightly linked your body, mind, and energy are.

How does all of this affect your learning? Think back to a time you had to learn something new. Maybe it was a dance step, an office or workplace procedure, a hobby skill, or a computer game. Maybe it was something you worked out yourself, or something you learned from a book or another person. Maybe you were all by yourself, or one-on-one with a teacher, or in a class full of other students.

What was the environment like? Was it noisy or quiet? Were you alone or with others? If you were with others, were they working on the same task as you, or were they doing something else? Was it easy to focus on what you were trying to do, or were there many distractions? How did your particular situation make it easier or more difficult to learn? What could have been changed to make it easier?

As you progress in the exercise, continue to observe your physical self, your energy states, and your states of consciousness. What are you like when you are happy, sad, excited, calm, nervous, powerful, edgy, or relaxed? How do these states feel energetically? Do you feel stuck, hyperactive, light-headed, firmly rooted, balanced, or disconnected? What is your energy state at a rock concert, as opposed to the symphony? At a car race or a flower show? A job interview or an intimate moment with someone you love?

Most importantly, notice how your body reacts to each energy state. Are you upright or slumped, tense or relaxed? Are your breaths shallow, or deep and slow? Experiment with changing your body and notice your reactions. What happens to a good mood if you deliberately slump down? What happens to a calm state if you begin rapid breathing?

You will learn that just as an actor takes on a role, you can take on an energy state by inducing the change through manipulation of your physical self. Act "as if"—and you can become it. With practice, you will be able to shift from state to state with fluid movement. Indeed, one of the classic definitions of magic is the ability to change your consciousness at will.

"Grounding" will give you a stasis or starting point from which energy changes can flow. We'll give you an exercise for that at the end of Chapter 4.

Part
II

Energies From
the
Environment

Chapter 3

Three Worlds and Five Elements

Indo-European Cosmology

Before we can understand the Elemental system that Western magicians and mystics have used for so many centuries, we first need to look at the common cosmological beliefs of the ancient Indo-European peoples. ("Cosmology" refers to people's theories about how the universe or cosmos was created and/or how it works now.) The Indo-Europeans were a motley assortment of tribes that existed 4,000–5,000 years ago in territories stretching from India to Europe and beyond, and who spoke related languages. Most Europeans, people living in the Indian subcontinent, and current inhabitants of the Americas are descended from these people, and speak languages that are rooted in the many languages they spoke.

These peoples thought of all reality as composed of what we could call three horizontal "worlds" (the land, the waters, and the sky) of organic beings, and three vertical "realms" (the Underworld, the middle realm of land/waters/sky, and the celestial realm of the sun, moon, and stars) of inorganic existence.

The three worlds were present in, or reflected by, the three realms. There existed a "this world" and "Otherworld" polarity between the places where mortal and immortal beings resided, which could be perceived in all the other worlds and realms. There was also a set of three "gateways" passing between all of them in the form of sacred fires, sacred wells, and sacred trees (sometimes mountains or big stones), which were said to grow at the center of all things.[1]

Each of the three worlds had particular animals, such as fish or birds, associated with it, as well as various spirits that we might call "nature spirits" today. In addition, certain wild and domesticated creatures came to symbolize various concepts—such as courage (lions), faithfulness (dogs), wisdom (salmon), cunning (foxes), nurturing (cows), as well as wildness (wolves) and domesticity (sheep). To these were added various mythical animals, such as dragons, gryphons, satyrs, fauns, and so on.

Trees, with their roots growing into the land, requiring waters for nourishment, and their branches growing up into the sky, symbolized all three worlds, and sometimes the three realms as well (as in the Baltic regions). Trees also had species-specific associations: Oaks were connected to clergy and matters of knowledge, strength, stability, trustworthiness, truth, and order. Yews and other evergreens were connected to warriors, the ancestors, and all matters related to the dead. Birches were connected to the producers (an Indo-European social caste), and matters related to fertility, pleasure, marriage, and so forth.[2] Of course, plants and animals also had their own spirits, as did particular places and even inanimate objects, whether natural or human made. We'll talk more about these ideas in later chapters, but for now it's sufficient to say that the cosmology of the three worlds and its attendant doctrines is one rich in organic metaphors.

To the ancient Indo-Europeans, including the Vedic/Indian peoples, the Iranians, the Hittites, the Greeks, the Romans, the Celts, the Slavs, the Norse, and the Germans, fire was seen as the tangible symbol of deities and other spirits. Tribes such as the Aryas of ancient India or the Gaels of Gaul and the British Isles, took their names (both meaning "shining ones") from the association of fire with deities, light, brightness, intelligence, creativity, beauty, and other valued concepts. Fire was present in all three worlds: on the land as wildfire or human hearths; in the waters as swamp lights; and in the sky as lightning. It was also thought to exist in the three realms: in the Underworld in the form of coal fires and burning lava; in the middle realm as it was in the three worlds; and in the celestial realm as the sun, moon, and stars. With their roots and branches extended to infinity, sacred trees were also metaphorically connected to the Underworld and the celestial realm. The waters of the sacred well could seen in this way as well, but neither the trees or the waters were as visibly ubiquitous as the sacred fire.

Perhaps this is why, when looking at the physical world around them, these ancient peoples tended to think in patterns of "three-plus-one"—that is, the land, the waters, and the sky (or sometimes the Underworld, the middle realm, and the celestial realm), plus fire. Interestingly, this pattern matched their social systems, which were originally composed of the three main classes or castes of producers, warriors, clergy, plus royalty (the tribal chieftains). So how did this three-plus-one pattern evolve into the modern magical and mystical cosmology of Air, Earth, Fire, Water, and Spirit, which is a system of "four-plus-one"?

An Elementary Theory

Ancient Greek philosophers from about 600 B.C.E. onward tried to figure out what primal substance or substances had given rise to the world as they knew it. They called each of these suggested substances *stoikheion*, meaning "a step or component part." This term became "elements" in English, from the Latin *elementum*, which the Romans used to translate the Greek term. The philosophers took the ancient Indo-European concepts of the three worlds plus fire, abstracted them into the concept of the Elements (Earth, Water, Air, and Fire), and then proceeded to argue over which one had given rise to the others.

One philosopher, Empedocles (490–430 B.C.E.), believed that everything in the universe was comprised of varying amounts of all four of these abstract concepts. Later, Aristotle (384–322 B.C.E.) furthered the abstraction by discussing these four Elements as representing combinations of the "specific being" or essence (from the Latin *essentia*, from *esse-*, meaning "to be") of two fundamental sets of polarities—hot and cold, and wet and dry. Thus, Earth was cold and dry, Water was cold and wet, Air was hot and wet, and Fire was hot and dry. Aristotle thought that there must be something that was beyond, or the origin of, these four essences (heat, cold, dryness, wetness) that would be a "quintessence" ("quint," meaning five), which he called the fifth Element of Aether.

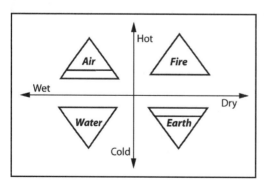

Figure 12: *The four classical Elements.*

In India, the clergy originally had a system of just three Elements or original substances— Earth, Water, and Fire. They also embraced the three-plus-one system centered on the three worlds. After encountering the Greek system around 400–500 C.E. (there was a lot of trade between India and the Mediterranean, and philosophers and clergy traveled in both directions), the Hindus added Air and Aether—which they called *Akasha*—as elements. The system was then brought back to Europe, where medieval clergy and magicians translated Akasha/Aether as "Spirit," and called it the fifth Element. By this time, the original Indo-European concept that land, waters, and sky represented organic realms of living beings, and Fire represented spirit, had been forgotten in Christendom, which preferred nature to be dead and exploitable, in keeping with the Christian theology and philosophy of the time. So, medieval and Renaissance magicians and mystics appropriated the expanded Greek Elements, often representing them by a five-pointed star of interlaced lines, now known as a pentagram (literally, "five lines").

It should be obvious that these mystical Elements are not the same thing as what modern scientists call "elements," although an argument can be made that they represent the states of matter. Thus, the Elements Earth, Water, Air, and Fire could be seen as the solid, liquid, gas, and plasma states respectively, while Spirit might represent the quantum field—or perhaps dark energy, if we want to annoy the physicists.[3] To keep matters clear in this book, we will capitalize the word "Elements," as well as their individual names, when we are speaking metaphysically, and leave it lowercase in scientific contexts.

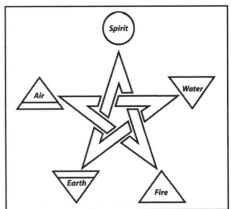

Figure 13: *The Elemental pentagram.*

Let's take a quick look at how the Elements are viewed in traditional Western and modern Neo-Pagan and New Age thought.

A Guided Tour of the Elements

Phaedra and Isaac both believe that it's a waste of (real) energy and the readers' time to continually reinvent the wheel, so we will quote in this section from two classics of magical literature, one old and one new. The first work, *The Magus*, was published in London in 1801 by Francis Barrett, F.R.C., one of the last of the "olde tyme" occultists (and a professional chemist). The book consists of what appears to be many years of collected notes on subjects then considered "occult," or hidden. Among these subjects included his theories of "natural magic," the secret properties of crystals and gemstones, magical potions, and many other such matters, including a great deal of discussion of the Elements. To get an idea of just how comprehensive Barrett's "theory of everything" was, we need only look at the book's full title:

THE MAGUS, OR CELESTIAL INTELLIGENCER; BEING A COMPLETE SYSTEM OF OCCULT PHILOSOPHY. IN THREE BOOKS; Containing the Antient [sic] and Modern Practice of the Cabalistic Art, Natural and Celestial Magic, &c.; shewing the wonderful Effects that may be performed by a Knowledge of the Celestial Influences, the occult Properties of Metals, Herbs, and Stones, AND THE APPLICATION OF ACTIVE TO PASSIVE PRINCIPLES. EXHIBITING THE SCIENCES OF NATURAL MAGIC; Alchymy, or Hermetic Philosophy; ALSO THE NATURE, CREATION, AND FALL OF MAN; His natural and supernatural Gifts; the magical Power inherent in the Soul, &c.; with a great Variety of rare Experiments in Natural Magic: THE CONSTELLATORY

PRACTICE, or TALISMANIC MAGIC; The Nature of the Elements. Stars, Planets, Signs, &c.; the Construction and Composition of all Sorts of Magic Seals, Images, Rings, Glasses, &c.; The Virtue and Efficacy of Numbers, Characters, and Figures, of good and evil Spirits. MAGNETISM, AND CABALISTICAL OR CEREMONIAL MAGIC; In which, the secret Mysteries of the Cabala are explained; the Operations of good and evil Spirits; all Kinds of Cabalistic Figures, Tables, Seals, and Names, with their Use, &c. THE TIMES, BONDS, OFFICES, AND CONJURATION OF SPIRITS. TO WHICH IS ADDED Biographia Antiqua, or the Lives of the most eminent Philosophers, Magi, &c. The Whole illustrated with a great Variety of CURIOUS ENGRAVINGS, MAGICAL AND CABALISTICAL FIGURES, &c.

Whew! No wonder later generations just called it *The Magus*.

A more recent classic (with a much shorter title) was written by Isaac's former wife, Wiccan priestess Deborah Lipp, and is titled *The Way of Four*. This book draws on the writings of many ancient and modern authors, and summarizes them clearly and succinctly. We can't recommend this book highly enough to readers interested in learning not just abstract ideas about the Elements, but practical ways to incorporate the Elements into their daily lives.

As we look at what these two authors have to say about the Elements, note that we have retained their own capitalization, but modernized Barrett's spelling and punctuation as needed for comprehension. We will insert any necessary explanatory notes in square brackets, and add our own two cent's worth afterwards. Barrett begins by describing the Elements:

There are four elements, the original grounds of all corporeal things, viz. [that is] fire, earth, water, and air, of which elements all inferior bodies are compounded; not by way of being heaped up together, but by transmutation and union; and when they are destroyed, they are resolved into elements. But there are none of the sensible [tangible] elements that are pure; but they are, more or less, mixed, and apt to be changed the one into the other: even as earth, being moistened and dissolved, becomes water, but the same being made thick and hard, becomes earth again; and being evaporated through heat it passes into air, and that being kindled into fire, and this being extinguished, into air again, but being cooled after burning, becomes earth again, or else stone, or sulfur; and this is clearly demonstrated by lightning. Now every one of these elements have two specific properties: the former whereof it retains as proper to itself; in the other, as a mean, it agrees with that which comes directly after it. For fire is hot and dry; earth, cold and dry; water, cold and moist; and air, hot and moist.[4]

And so in this manner the elements, according to two contrary qualities, are opposite one to the other: as fire to water, and earth to air. Likewise, the elements are contrary one to the other in another account: two are heavy, as earth and water—and the others are light, as fire and air; therefore the Stoics called the former passives but the latter actives. And Plato distinguishes them after another manner, and assigns to each of them three qualities, viz. to the fire, brightness, thinness, and motion; to the earth, darkness, thickness, and quietness;

and, according to these qualities, the elements of fire and earth are contrary. Now the other elements borrow their qualities from these, so that the air receives two qualities from the fire, thinness and motion; and the earth one, viz. darkness. In like manner water receives two qualities of the earth, darkness and thickness; and the fire one, viz. motion. But fire is twice as thin as air, thrice more moveable, and four times brighter; the air is twice more bright, thrice more thin, and four times more moveable. Therefore, as fire is to air, so is air to water, and water to the earth; and again, as the earth is to the water, so is water to air, and air to fire. And this is the root and foundation of all bodies, natures, and wonderful works; and he who can know, and thoroughly understand these qualities of the elements, and their mixtures, shall bring to pass wonderful and astonishing things in magic. Now each of these elements have a threefold consideration, so that the number of four may make up the number of twelve."[5]

We can see here Barrett's attempt to discuss ancient, prescientific concepts in 18th-century scientific language, a pattern that will hold throughout his book. By way of contrast, let's see how Lipp introduces the concept of the Elements:

In Wicca and much of the occult, the four elements of Fire, Water, Air, and Earth describe the universe and everything in it. Everything can be understood as taking part in one or more elements. Everything that is whole contains all four, and can be understood more deeply by dividing it into four and viewing it through that lens. The elements are the building blocks of creation; they are the beginning of *things*. The undifferentiated void that preceded creation had no elements, or, to put it another way, all elements were One. But creation—things, reality—consists of the elements. From a scientific point of view, the periodic table of the elements describes the building blocks of the universe, and the modern magician doesn't reject science. But from a magical point of view, both simplicity and symbolism call for only four elements. The four elements give us a way of thinking about the world. They give us a structured approach to knowing the unknowable. They provide us with a system of interrelations, and magic is all about interrelations.[6]

Clearly Lipp agrees with Barrett when he states that magicians approve of mainstream science but choose to differ with it for philosophical and practical magical reasons. The fact is that there are times when thinking in terms of mystical Elements, rather than chemical or physical elements, is more useful to a magician or mystic. Isaac and Phaedra agree with them both, though we will point out here that, despite the opinions of Barrett and the older occultists, it is very clear that Elemental energies have little to do with those studied by physicists—at least at first glance.

Earth

Barrett tells us:

Now the basis and foundation of all the elements is the earth; for that is the object, subject, and receptacle of all celestial rays and influences: in it are contained the seeds, and seminal virtues of all things; and therefore, it is said to be animal, vegetable, and mineral. It, being made fruitful by the other elements and the heavens, brings forth all things of itself. It receives the abundance of all things, and is, as it were, the first fountain from whence all things spring; it is the centre, foundation, and mother of all things. Take as much of it as you please, separated, washed, depurated [purified], and subtilized [ground fine], and if you let it lie in the open air a little while, it will, being full and abounding with heavenly virtues, of itself bring forth plants, worms, and other living things;[7] also stones, and bright sparks of metals. In it are great secrets: if, at any time it shall be purified, by the help of fire, and reduced into its simple nature by a convenient washing, it is the first matter of our creation, and the truest medicine that can restore and preserve us.[8]

Lipp writes:

Earth is the substance of the body of our Mother, Gaia, the Earth Herself. Earth is manifest in all things that are solid, or fertile, or both: rocks, green fields, rolling hills, and soil. Caves and other buried places are quintessentially[9] Earthy....A human being's Earth is her *body*. From Earth comes solidity, stability, and commitment. We call Earth our home, both the home of all life that is Mother Earth, and the house we live in. By extension, Earth is hearth and family and all those qualities that make us feel at home....To be an Earthy person is to be pragmatic, realistic, and tactile....Earth is that deep, solid, immobile place, both in the negative sense of stubborn and in the positive sense of patient.[10]

Water

When explaining Water, Barrett writes:

There is so great a necessity of water, that without it nothing can live—no herb nor plant whatsoever without the moistening of water, can bring forth; in it is the seminary [seed] virtue of all things, especially of animals, whose seed is manifestly waterish. The seeds, also, of trees and plants, although they are earthy, must, notwithstanding, of necessity be rotted in water before they can be fruitful; whether they be imbibed with the moisture of the earth, or with dew, or rain, or any other water that is on purpose put to them.[11]

Barrett then goes on at great length about the spiritual power of Water for cleansing, healing, and blessing purposes, and quotes the Christian Bible for his examples (as he later does for Fire).

Lipp writes:

There are myriad natural forms of water, including not just the sea, but every body of water from a little creek to the Great Lakes. Water is also found in our bodies: in the clichéd "blood, sweat, and tears," in mother's milk, and, perhaps most importantly, in amniotic fluid....Since all bodies of water have tides, the Moon is also associated with water, and many lunar qualities are also Water qualities....The personal quality of Water is *feeling*. Emotion flows, following its own path, which may meander. Emotion runs deep, with mysteries not visible on the surface....The Moon and Water are the menstrual cycle, and Water is childbirth as well, making Water perhaps the most feminine of elements. Since Moon phases are cyclic, ending where they begin and beginning where they end, it makes sense that Water is also associated with death, and it's not surprising that many people's folklore depicts death as a passage over water. To make the cycle complete, Hindus refer to rebirth as an ocean. All these things...combine to associate Water with dreams and the subconscious, and from there to altered states of consciousness in general....Watery people are weepy and overflowing with feeling. They are dramatic, sensual, and otherworldly.[12]

Air

When explaining Air, Barrett writes:

This is a vital spirit passing through all beings—giving life and subsistence to all things—moving and filling all things. Hence it is that the Hebrew doctors reckon it not amongst the elements; but count it as a medium, or glue, joining things together, and as the resounding spirit of the world's instrument. It immediately receives into itself the influence of all celestial bodies, and then communicates them to the other elements, as also to all mixed bodies. Also, it receives into itself, as if it were a divine looking-glass, the species [character or kind] of all things, as well natural as artificial; as also of all manner of speeches, and retains them; and carrying them with it, and entering into the bodies of men, and other animals, through their pores, makes an impression upon them, as well when they are asleep as when they are awake, and affords matter for divers strange dreams and divinations. Hence, they say, it is that a man, passing by a place where a man was slain, or the carcass newly hid, is moved with fear and dread; because the air, in that place, being full of the dreadful species of man-slaughter,[13] doth, being breathed in, move and trouble the spirit of the man with the like species; whence it is that he becomes afraid. For every thing that makes a sudden impression astonishes Nature.[14]

Barrett then goes on to associate what we would call telepathy with "species" (ideas) being carried by the Element of Air, mentioning mirages and cloud images as functions of this Element. He also discusses ancient methods of transmitting information through moonlight, ending by saying this:

And all these things, and many more, and much greater than these, are grounded in the very nature of the air, and have their reasons and causes declared in mathematics and optics. And as these resemblances are reflected back to the sight, so also are they, sometimes, to the hearing, as is manifest in echo. But there are many more secret arts than these, and such whereby any one may, at a remarkable distance, hear, and understand distinctly, what another speaks or whispers.[15]

We can see here the inception of what would become a standard Western association between Air and communication—both normal and paranormal—as well as intellect and mental skills in general. In this, Lipp agrees with Barrett:

In the natural world, Air is associated most closely with the sky, wind, and clouds. Birds of all kinds belong to this element....In a person, Air is associated with thought and with the intellect....Ideas are said to come from Air, as is inspiration, a word that also means "to breathe in." Logic and scholarship are Air functions, which is perhaps why academics are said to live in ivory towers as opposed to ivory basements. People who spend all their time thinking "have their heads in the clouds," and if they're "airheads," they mistake imagination for real life and are impractical.[16]

Fire

When explaining Fire, Barrett states:

Fire, in all things, and through all things, comes and goes away bright; it is in all things bright, and at the same time occult, and unknown. When it is by itself (no other matter coming to it, in which it should manifest its proper action) it is boundless and invisible; of itself sufficient for every action that is proper to it; itself is one, and penetrates through all things; also spread abroad in the heavens, and shining. But in the infernal place, straitened [sic], dark, and tormenting; and in the midway it partakes of both. It is in stones, and is drawn out by the stroke of the steel; it is in earth, and causes it, after digging up, to smoke; it is in water, and heats springs and wells; it is in the depths of the sea, and causes it, being tossed with the winds, to be hot; it is in the air, and makes it (as we often see) to burn. And all animals, and all living things whatsoever, as also vegetables, are preserved by heat; and every thing that lives, lives by reason of the enclosed heat. The properties of the fire that is above, are heat, making all things fruitful; and a celestial light, giving life to all things. The properties of the infernal fire are a parching heat, consuming all things; and darkness; making all things barren. The celestial and bright fire drives away spirits of darkness; also, this our fire, made with wood, drives away the same, in as much as it hath an analogy with, and is the vehiculum [vehicle] of, that superior light; as also of him who saith, "I am the light of the world," which is true fire—the Father of lights, from whom every good thing that is given comes; sending forth the light of his fire, and communicating it first to the sun and the rest of the celestial bodies, and by these, as by mediating instruments, conveying that light into our fire.[17]

Leaving the overt Christian theology aside, it is clear that there is a remnant here of the older idea that Fire is Spirit, and as such can literally convey Spirit to us through our candles, torches, and hearth fires.

Lipp writes:

In nature, Fire is *itself*, first and foremost. Fire has always been set aside from the other elements, because Fire alone has no natural home on the earth; Air has the sky, Water the sea, and Earth the land, but only Fire stands apart from geography...In nature, Fire is the outsider; it is out of control, and it conforms to no known rules[18]....The place Fire is most connected to is the desert....Other natural things associated with Fire either burn, like chilies and cumin, or are red or especially orange-colored, like fire opals....The personal quality of Fire is *will*....Willfulness burns hot, and the will to get things done is a spark that ignites. Temper is also associated with Fire, a fiery person is a "hothead," and lust is Fiery—you burn with desire. All of these things are closely associated with the life force itself, the spark within that fills us with life. For that reason, healing is a thing of fire; a person who is losing his spark needs Fire magic to reignite him.[19]

In summary, we see that Earth is the Element of the body and all that is physical, tangible, solid, and "real." We are being "earthy" when we revel in our physicality. When we are being practical, we are "down to earth." Earth, too, is mystery and wildness—the leaping stag, deserted mountains, the vitality of living, and the secrets of the hidden cave and virgin forest. Because of their solidity, many hoofed animals, such as cattle and goats, are associated with the Element of Earth.

Earth can represent both the concept of physical matter and the ground upon which we stand. Being metaphysically or spiritually "grounded" can also mean draining off excess energy *into* the ground, as with a lightning rod, or being nourished by pulling energy *up* from the ground, as a plant would do. Either way, the Earth Element is used as an essential concept in grounding meditations and rituals.

Water is the Element of the unconscious, the ocean of dreams, and the depths of our emotions. These are the healing waters of love and hope, the salt sea from which all life springs, and the womb waters that hold safe that which is not yet born. Dive deep, we say, into the well of the heart.

Air is the Element of the mind, representing our ability to think and to discriminate, to know and to understand. The breath of life, as Lipp pointed out, is literally "inspiration." This is the place of beginnings, new ideas that come "like a breath of fresh air."

Fire is the Element of energy, will, and transformation. This is the passion that pushes us, and the force with which we can transform ourselves and the world.

But what of Spirit? Both authors speak of spiritual matters throughout their books, but not in the concentrated way they did when discussing the other Four Elements. Suffice it to say that Spirit is the Element of ultimate identity, and, many mystics believe, of ultimate reality. It exists everywhere and nowhere; it cannot be measured or its motion mapped. Yet, when its power and influence depart, we are metaphorically or literally dead.

Cosmic Cubbyholes

However it originated and developed over the past 15 centuries or so, the idea of the Five Elements as it exists today is primarily used as the basis of a core Western "system of correspondences," which plays a part in other systems such as astrology and the tarot. Systems of correspondences or associations give us a framework for categorizing objects and experiences according to how alike or unlike they are. Many modern Western magicians and mystics believe that everything can be categorized by how well it corresponds to the qualities of Elemental energy represented by Air, Earth, Fire, Water, and Spirit. You may have noticed how often Lipp uses the phrase, "is associated with," in her Elemental descriptions. This is because for most moderns, the Elements are more useful for their correspondences than for their abstract philosophical meanings.

Things that are similar attract and support each other. In magical terms, this refers to the laws of similarity and contagion discussed in Chapter 2. Like emotions, magical similarity is contagious: just as laughter draws more laughs to it (while a frown encourages frowns), anything that corresponds to a particular Element draws or attracts things that have similar qualities. Thus, the more we understand about the tangible and intangible qualities of an Element, the more we can wield the principles of similarity and contagion in our Elemental magic.

Here's an example: The Element of Fire is associated with the tangible quality of heat, as well as the intangible qualities of courage and passion. If we want to work magic geared toward the intangible qualities of passion or courage, we would enhance the effectiveness of our ritual by including items that embody the tangible quality of heat. Heat is associated with hot peppers, roaring furnaces, high summer, and the color red; hence, all of these things have Fire correspondences, and therefore have something in common with everything else that corresponds to Fire. So, in order to align ourselves most powerfully with our desired result of passion or courage, we surround ourselves with things that have a fiery nature: we eat spicy food, we wear red, we use images of furnaces in our visualizations, or we do our ritual at high noon on the summer solstice.

Because everything that exists corresponds with one of the Elements, the presence of all four Elements together symbolizes completeness. Thus, when we call Air, Earth, Fire, Water, and Spirit to be present in our rituals or meditations, we are calling upon all there is in the universe (the "macrocosm") to be in attendance and to help us in our work. On page 114 is a brief summary of some typical, but not universal or absolute, Elemental correspondences as used by most modern Western metaphysical and esoteric movements.

Many mystics and magicians believe that we, as individuals, are "microcosms" of the larger universe, or "macrocosm"—a concept summed up in the phrase, "as above, so below." One of the ways in which this principle is thought to be manifested is in the notion that each one of us is composed of the five Elements. Different parts of us correspond to different Elements, and the whole self contains them all. Thus, when we evoke the Elements in a ceremonial space, we are also calling *ourselves* to

Element	Air	Fire	Water	Earth	Spirit
Direction	East	South	West	North	Center/Circumference
Intangibles	Inspiration, Creative Breakthroughs, Beginnings	Energy, Passion, Courage, Determination, Transformation, Purification, Peak Experiences	Love, Hope, Caring, Compassion, Fear, Dreams, Change, Flow, Ebb, Gate to the Summerland	Concreteness, Reality, Stability, Money, Housing	Centrality, Encompassment, Merging
Mystical Body	Mental	Causal	Astral	Physical	Soul, Astral Self
Human Nature	Mind, Intellect, Breath, Voice, Hearing, Smell, Birth, Childhood	True Will, Sexuality, Blood, Sight, Prime of Life	Emotions, Unconscious, Heart, Womb, Aging, Death	Body, Touch, Afterlife	
Natural World	Spring, Sunrise, First Crescent, Waxing Moon, Clouds, Wind, Windy Places, High Cliffs, Open Fields	Summer, Noon, Full Moon, Heat, Deserts, Dry Places, Cacti, Peppers, Volcanoes, Flames	Autumn, Twilight, Waning Moon, Lakes, Rivers, Oceans, Rainfall, Dew, Water Plants	Winter, Midnight, Dark of the Moon, Mountains, Forests, Caves, Crystals, Precious Gems and Metals, Land Plants	Seasonal Cusps, Twilight/Dawn, Noon/Midnight
Animals	Birds, Bats, Feathers	Lizards, Big Cats	Fish, Dolphins, Seals, Whales, Snakes	Stags, Bulls, Badgers, Bears, Wolves, Snakes	Totem Animals, Spirit Guides
Mythical Beasts	Dragons, Harpies	Dragons, Phoenix	Dragons, Sea Serpents, Mermaids	Dragons, Satyrs, Fauns	Unicorns
Color	Yellow, Violet, grey, Sky-blue	Red, Orange, Gold	Blue, Sea-green, Purple, Silver	Green, Brown, Black, Gold	White, Grey
Magical Tools	Athame, Dagger, Incense, Sword	Wand, Candle, Flaming Cauldron	Cup, Cauldron, Mirror	Pentacle, Salt, Oil	Bell
Astrological Sign	Gemini, Libra, Aquarius	Aries, Leo, Sagittarius	Cancer, Scorpio, Pisces	Taurus, Virgo, Capricorn	
Elemental Beings	Sylphs (ruled by Peralda)	Salamanders (ruled by Djinn)	Undines (ruled by Neknar or Niksa)	Gnomes (ruled by Ghob)	

Table 1: *Some Elemental correspondences.*

be fully present. For example, when the officer of the East in a ritual is opening the portal to (psychically connecting with) the Element of Air, we should each evoke our own "Airy" selves, allowing our breath, intellect, and inspiration to awaken, to open up, and to be fully present.

The powers and influences of the Elements are often personified as Elemental beings, or just "Elementals," and are grouped according to kind. In traditional Western magic and mysticism, each group is ruled by a king, whom ceremonial magicians bargain with for particular goals. Whether these Elementals and their rulers are real beings in any absolute sense or not is irrelevant; what matters is that it works very well to think about them in this way, just as the magical law of personification states. We'll discuss working with Elementals further in Chapter 9.

When most modern people talk about using "Elemental energies," however, they are dealing more with states of consciousness or intellectual and artistic systems of correspondences, than with anything that a physicist would recognize as "energetic." How do you get into these states of consciousness? By doing elementary exercises, of course!

Most modern Western magical systems rely heavily on the four- or five-Element system, and they each have practices to hone awareness of the energies of these Elements. They know that the more you are aware of an Elemental energy (a particular ASC), the more likely it is that you will be able to manipulate it. Although every system will have its own way of going about this, the systems of Elemental correspondences are used to enhance the practitioner's ability to access the unique "flavor" of each element, as well heighten his or her sensitivity to them. Our Elemental exercises take advantage of the ubiquity of

Elemental correspondences in so many systems of energy manipulation and magic.

Correspondences, as you may recall, are tangible, understandable embodiments of the energies of the Elements. They are terrific tools to use when you are seeking to sensitize yourself to each Element's unique energies. Use the most essential or obvious correspondence to hone your awareness of these distinctive energies. Eventually, you'll build a "personal data bank" of corresponding experiences from which you can draw. How does this work? Let's say you wish to strengthen your connection to the Element of Water. Today, you happen to be wading in the surf. As you splash, concentrate on the experience, really noticing details such as what the water feels like on your skin, what the sensation of the waves lapping on your legs is like, and what the waves look like. Feel the temperature of the water. Smell the air. Hear the gulls. Knock the sand out of your sneakers.

Later, you may find yourself in a Wiccan circle and being asked to call the "Quarter" of Water. As you stand facing the West, you could imagine the feel, the smells, the sounds, and the sensations of standing ankle deep in the ocean. The literal memory of the water shifts your own energy to a more "watery" place, and it becomes easier to be a channel for the energy of Water. When you consciously choose to remember all the specifics of your experience, the memory becomes a resource you can draw upon. When you remember the earlier experience of being connected to Water, you are able to experience it again, aligning yourself much more quickly and successfully with the Element's characteristic energy.

Now, let's say that when wading in the water, you also deliberately wore a blue shirt or blue robe or a ring with dolphins on it, and you scooped up some of the water in a special cup or bottle. Any and all of these things can serve as a trigger to access the experience again. If you wear the ring and the robe into your circle, and hold the cup of water while calling your Quarter, the memory will be even more intense in the presence of those tangible reminders.

You can also set these items apart and dedicate them to a specific use in ritual. For example, wear the blue garment or the dolphin ring, or use the cup or water bottle only when you are consciously working to access the energy of Water. Reserving their use for only one purpose will imbue them with a special quality, which will enhance their ability to trigger your memories and hence your experience of Water energy.

Perhaps now you understand why many magical and energy systems emphasize setting aside specific garments and accessories to be used only in ceremony or ritual. The very act of donning the garments triggers a change in your mystical energies. Much like an actor donning his or her character's costume, you begin to become something other than your everyday self.

Exercise 2:
Meeting the Elements

We're presenting this exercise in two forms, each with four parts (one for each Element, if you haven't already guessed). Neither exercise is dependent on the other, so you can do either one or both, but you may find that doing them in sequence is helpful. The exercises themselves are described first, and at the end of each you'll find some suggestions for Elemental correspondences to use (plus many more elsewhere in this chapter). Be aware that both versions are, in essence, putting you and your awareness out of balance. Accordingly, you'll probably be happiest if you go through the entire cycle of four. And remember to take the time you need at the end of each individual section to return yourself to a more balanced state.

Level I: Awareness of the Elements

For this exercise, you will be increasing your awareness of each Element by finding it in your everyday life. No special equipment is required, only open eyes and conscious observation. For each Element in turn, look around your environment and note everything and anything that corresponds to, or could be associated with, that Element. Engage all your senses in the hunt for the Element, including touch, smell, taste, and hearing. Here are some examples: Water goes in a cup. Look around your room—how many cup or bowl shapes do you see? Trees grow in the Earth. How many things made of wood (or stone) can you find? Many things are conveyed through the Air. What do you hear and smell? Think creatively. Although Fire is hot, the refrigerator might yield some spicy foods.

Limit yourself to one Element at a time, and decide in advance how long the exercise will last. We recommend that you concentrate on each Element one hour per day, one full day, or up to one full week at most. If you choose an hour, do each Element on four days in succession. You may wish to record your observations in a journal.

Level II: Immersion in the Elements

For this exercise, you will be immersing yourself in the Elements, one by one, by surrounding yourself with objects and experiences that correspond with them. Incorporate each Element in turn into every aspect of your day. Dress in Elemental colors. Eat food and drink beverages that could be associated with your Element. Choose activities related to the Element; for example, go swimming or skydiving, or plant a tree. Watch a movie that relates to your Element, say, an action flick for Fire, or a chick flick for Water. If you used a journal for Level 1 of the exercise, refer to it for further inspiration. Recommended duration: one full day, one full week, one full month, or one complete season per Element.

A few suggested correspondences to watch for and use:

➤ **Clothing**

✦ Air: Thin, floaty fabrics in pale colors, light linens, mesh, netting.

✦ Fire: Bright colors (especially reds and oranges), shiny or metallic fabrics.

✦ Water: Blue and muted tones, flowing silks or crepes.

✦ Earth: Wool, denim, or leather in green, brown, black, or white.

➤ **Food**

✦ Air: Carbonated beverages, whipped cream, mousse, meringues, poultry.

✦ Fire: Hot drinks, spicy tomato juice, anything with hot peppers.

✦ Water: All beverages (especially cool ones), soups, juicy fruits, fish.

✦ Earth: Frozen drinks, heavy stews, game meats, fresh or raw vegetables.

➤ **Magical**

✦ Air: Swords, knives, sharp edges, birds, feathers, incense.

✦ Fire: Flames, candles, staves, rods.

✦ Water: Cups, bowls, cauldrons, fish, flowing water.

✦ Earth: Pentacle, stones, forests.

➤ **Timing**

✦ Air: Begin at dawn, spring equinox, or the heliacal new moon.

✦ Fire: Begin at noon, summer solstice, or the full moon.

✦ Water: Begin at sunset, autumnal equinox, or the waning moon.

✦ Earth: Begin at midnight, winter solstice, or the dark of the moon.

(Note: the suggested timing for these exercises may be inconvenient. This is another case of "do as you are able." However, by inconveniencing yourself, you are sending the message to your inner self that the activity is important enough to justify the inconvenience. In other words, if you make it more difficult for yourself, you just might get more out of it.)

Chapter 4

Cosmic and Earth Energies

Lunar and Solar Rhythms

Mystics and magicians sometimes speak of working with the energies of the solar and lunar tides—that is, the time of day, the season, or the phase of the moon. The energy during the time of the full moon, for instance, is different from that of the dark of the moon or the waxing moon. The energy of summer is different from that of winter. The energy of midnight is different from that of the morning. What are these people talking about?

Earth critters—and human beings are but glorified critters (sorry)—have been programmed through millions of years of evolution to respond to natural events and natural rhythms rather than clocks or calendars. Most of us get sleepy at night and feel perkier when the sun shines, and these feelings represent real changes in body energy. Rainy days really *do* get you down. A full moon lights up the night, but during the dark of the moon, it is really, really dark out there (at least if you live in the country). Physiologists call our responses to these regular changes in light and weather our circadian rhythms (from the

Latin, *circa* for circle, and *dies* for day). As modern people, we don't really understand this; we're too used to artificial light, mechanical timekeeping, and weird quirks such as daylight saving time. High noon is supposed to be the sun at its highest point, not the two clock hands pointing up, remember?[1]

Circadian rhythms and the natural phenomena that cause them are still very much a part of our lives. Many people get migraines from extreme changes in barometric pressure. Others spend the winter experiencing SAD (seasonal affective disorder), reacting negatively to the lack of natural light during the short winter days. Shift workers have a terrible time constantly adjusting their sleep cycles to the demands of the clock rather than the rhythms of the sun.

The energy practitioner, if he or she wants to work with natural rhythms, must be aware of what the rhythms really are. Times and seasons should be your local times and seasons. Noon should be determined by the sun's position, not by a timepiece. Midnight is the midpoint of the hours of darkness, and winter solstice is the shortest day and longest night—all of which may mean very little if you live near the equator, where all days and nights are pretty much the same length. The practitioner can also take advantage of obvious human rhythms. When most people are sleeping late at night, for example, there is less psychic "static." The practitioner can also tap into communal energy—knowing that others are doing something at 12 midnight may be as mystically, magically, psychically, or spiritually useful as the energies themselves that occur during this time. (What kinds of energies are we talking about so far in this chapter? Physical, psychological, and even metaphorical energies—all of which can affect a person's mystical energies, as well as those of the environment in which he or she is working.)

One of the unfortunate side effects of modern life is the loss of natural light. Many of us are forced to spend our days in windowless environments, so that we hardly see the sun. Light pollution at night drowns out starlight. How many of us have seen the Milky Way lately—or ever? How many of us can remember a sky so dense with stars they were like sand on a beach? The phases of the moon mean little to folks who live in the land of streetlights. The difference between the dark of the moon and the moon at its fullness is difficult to understand under those streetlights, but once you step away from their glare, the moon reveals herself in all her mystery. The dark of the moon is a very dark night indeed, while the full moon is bright enough to cast a shadow—have you ever seen your moon shadow (let alone been followed by it)?

The seasons of the sun also have a powerful effect upon us. No matter where you live on the planet, day becomes night and night becomes day. Our biorhythms respond to light and darkness in profound ways. It's much easier to sleep in a darkened room, and it's easier to wake when the sun rises before you do.

As we move toward the north and south and away from the equator, the seasons become more pronounced, and the lengths of days change as the solar year progresses. In the North American Midwest, where Phaedra spent much of her early magical career, she would dread the winter months that kept her indoors from before the dawn to after dusk. Each year, the first day she left the office while light was still in the sky (in that part of the world, around the beginning of February), it felt like a holiday.

Following are explanations of some of the physical and mystical energy characteristics of typical natural events, beginning with the lunar cycles.

New Moon/Dark of the Moon

A new moon occurs when the moon is blocked from reflecting the rays of the sun by the position of the Earth, which is exactly opposite its position when the moon is full. For approximately three days, or rather, nights, the moon is not visible in the sky. When there is no moon at night, it is very, very dark! On the upside, you can see lots of stars. On the downside, it's difficult to see where you're going—thus the classic narrative device of travelers waiting for the full moon for easy nighttime travel, or the dark of the moon for hidden travel. It may seem obvious to state just how dark it is during a new moon, but for those of us (and we are legion) who have always known streetlights and other forms of artificial light at night, it's often difficult to imagine. In fact, with the ever-increasing light pollution from our cities and suburbs, we may be creating a world in which night will never be truly dark again—a great loss for stargazers and other nocturnal critters!

The dark of night can be used energetically for secret, private, or introspective magic. Banishing, hexing, cursing, sending negative energy—all of these are associated with the dark of the moon. Some of this may sound grim, but context, as always, is everything. Healing is also associated with the energy of the dark moon, when one can banish illness or hex a tumor. Meditation or other introspective arts are also enhanced by the quiet darkness of a moonless night.

The new moon time and date listed in calendars, almanacs, and astrological reference tables is the approximate midpoint of the three dark nights, and exactly opposite the midpoint of the full moon in the 29 and one-quarter day lunar cycle.

New Moon/Heliacal Moon   *Diana's Bow*

As the moon moves around the Earth and catches the light of the sun once more, it is visible as a thin crescent, low on the horizon in the western sky right after sunset. This first crescent is the *heliacal* new moon (taken from *Helios*, the Greek sun god). Do not confuse the heliacal new moon, which is visible, with the astronomical or astrological new moon, which is not. Being able to calculate the exact midpoint of the dark nights (180 degrees away from the exact midpoint of the full moon) was not as interesting to our ancestors as what was actually going on in the sky.

According to lunar calendars, the new month begins and ends with the heliacal new moon. For example, the Islamic month of fasting, Ramadan, does not end until the next crescent is visible. Unfortunately for the fasters, overcast skies could extend the month indefinitely! But creative thinking solved that problem for modern Muslims. It is not specified who needs to see the new crescent, just that it needs to be seen. Therefore, worshipers in one mosque can telephone those at another mosque where the skies are clear. When the sighting is confirmed, the new month begins and the fasting is over.

The heliacal new moon will often be visible on the night after the date the new moon is listed in the calendars and almanacs. However, the vagaries of weather conditions and landscape features may make it visible sooner in one place than in another. If you are looking across flat, open land, you may be able to see the crescent a night or two sooner than if your view were blocked by mountains, hills, trees, or buildings.

The energy of the heliacal new moon is that of beginnings. Therefore, it's a great time to start projects, or add a burst of energy to continuing ones. Healings at this time might focus on increasing good health, rather than banishing illness.

Waxing Moon

From the day of the heliacal new moon, the size of the visible moon increases every night. The time of increase, approximately 13 days, is called the "waxing" (growing) of the moon. The energies of the waxing moon are used, reasonably enough, for increase and expansion. For example, you might use the growing energy to boost an immune system during a healing. It's also a great time to continue the projects begun during the heliacal new moon.

Full Moon

Imagine a night with no street lights, no lights spilling from any window, and no headlights from any passing cars. Imagine going out on such a night with nothing but the light of the moon alone—so dark in the shadows, yet so much light you can read by it and see your own shadow, your moon shadow. This is the magic of the full moon.

A full moon occurs when the moon is completely illuminated by the sun. The full moon time given in calendars and almanacs is the midpoint of the lunar cycle, exactly opposite from the dark of the moon or new moon. Strictly speaking, this midpoint marks the exact moment that the moon will wax no more and begin to wane, but the moon usually appears full to the naked eye for three nights—the official calendar and almanac date, the night before, and the night after. For the purposes of this book, all three of these nights contain full moon energy.

Covens and other sorts of magical working groups, such as healing circles, frequently meet during the full moon. In fact, a famous Wiccan text, the *Charge of the Goddess*, which has its roots in the material folklorist Charles Leland published at the turn of the previous century, exhorts followers: "Once in a month and better it be when the Moon is full, ye shall meet in some secret place and adore the spirit of Me who is Queen of all Witcheries." One could speculate that full moon meetings began in the way-back-when simply because people could see at night to get to them. (Speculation, of course, means that it sounds reasonable, even if there is no evidence that it *is* reasonable.) Let's speculate instead that energy workers meet at the full moon because that is when lunar energy at its highest point. You can use it for anything that needs a big boost or a good kick, or bring to a climax or finish whatever you started at the heliacal new moon.

Waning Moon

Over a period of about 10 days, when the moon is past full but before it has disappeared from the sky altogether, we say that the moon is waning. Energetically, this is a time of decrease and diminishment. Waning moons are great times for winding down and finishing up. As during the dark of the moon, it also is a time of hexing or banishing. Healers could use this time to banish illness or diminish a tumor, with the final kick given during the dark of the moon. Then we're right back where we were 29 and one-quarter days ago, and the lunar cycle starts over again.

Riding Our Solar Cycles

Now let's take a look at the solar cycles. The Earth takes a lot longer (more than 365 days) to move around the sun than the moon takes to move around the Earth. Thus, most solar effects last longer, and the solar energy cycles can be used over a longer period than the lunar ones. Moreover, where you live affects the sun's energy more than the moon's. How far away you are from the equator, and whether you are north or south of it, greatly affects the amount of solar energy (light) that hits the ground.

The equator is the line that marks the place at the Earth's circumference that is equidistant from both poles. The sun's rays hit the equator more consistently and more strongly than anywhere else on the planet. This is where we will always find the richest plant growth, and with rich plant life, of course, comes correspondingly rich critter life, too. Despite the proliferation of biological life, however, not much happens there in the way of solar cycles. The moon waxes and wanes, but the length of day and night stay pretty much the same. (Equal, equator—get it?) Thus, the seasons tend to be based on rainfall patterns rather than varying light amounts.

Move north or south and this changes. The tilt of the Earth puts some parts of the planet nearer or farther from the sun at different times in the Earth's orbit (the solar year, or the length of time needed for one complete circuit of the sun). The change in the length of days, which changes how much solar energy hits the ground, is what gives us our seasons.

If you are far enough north or south to have seasons, the most dramatic markers of the solar seasons are the solstices and equinoxes. The equinoxes occur when day and night are equal in length. For a day or so, wherever you are, you too can be equatorial! The solstices mark the days when the sun reaches its highest or lowest point in the midday sky. At these extremes, the hours of daylight will be at their maximum or minimum, giving us the longest and shortest days of the year, respectively, and the corresponding shortest and longest nights. As we move closer to either pole, these extremes become increasingly dramatic.

In Northern Europe, or the southernmost part of South America, the summer solstice sun may remain just barely beneath the horizon so that the night is never completely dark. At winter solstice in Antarctica, on the other hand, the sun may never rise above the horizon for weeks or months on end—there's a longest night for you!

Many cultures—ours in the United States included—use the solstices and equinoxes to mark the official transition from one season to another. But they have also been used to mark the middle of seasons—thus "midsummer" for the summer solstice, and "midwinter" for the night of the winter solstice. Among Wiccans, Druids, and some other Earth Religionists, the start and end of the seasons are designated by the "cross-quarter" days, so called because they fall (roughly or precisely, depending upon one's denomination and/or personal preferences) halfway between the solstices and equinoxes, which effectively separate the year into quarters.

Of course, depending on where you live, your weather may not reflect Western culture's classic four seasons. You may have two seasons, rainy and dry, as is found in most of the tropics, or three, as in ancient Egypt's seasons of growth, harvest, and flood. Our advice is to use the seasons you have, as they will be the most relevant energies for you.

Now let's look at the solar and seasonal energies you're most likely to encounter.

Spring Equinox

The astrological year begins with the spring equinox, 24 hours of equal day and night when the sun enters the astrological[2] sign of Aries. From this day forward, the days will be longer than the nights. In this context, spring might be thought of as parallel to the waxing moon. Increase is the name of the game, but the energies of the equinox itself, as a time of equilibrium, can be used for any purpose that requires balance or the restoration of balance.

Summer Solstice

Summer solstice energy is the year's equivalent to the full moon. Heat and light are at their peak during this longest day of the year. The night, of course, is correspondingly the shortest one of the year. Depending on where you are, it might be very short indeed. There is much lore connected with this night, especially in Northern Europe, where the night never really arrives. It is in this ambiguous space, not really day and not really night, where magic traditionally happens. Thus we have Shakespeare's *A Midsummer Night's Dream*, Bergman's *Smiles of a Summer Night*, and Sondheim's *A Little Night Music*, in which the night smiles upon fools and lovers both.

Because summer solstice represents the peak of solar power in both the literal and the metaphorical sense, energy workers can use its power to shine the full energy of the sun on their efforts. The other side of solstice is the change it heralds; from this point on, the days get shorter and the nights get longer.

Autumnal Equinox

This equinox represents the turning point between day and night. Again, day and night are equal, so the energies of balance are easy to access. At the same time, fall is coming with its growing darkness. The year itself is waning, and the nights to follow will be longer than the days to come. Gardens will wither and leaves fall. Farmers gather their crops and retreat indoors, bears retreat to their dens, and bats and groundhogs go into hibernation. As with the similar lunar energies of the waning and dark of the moon, these are the energies of decrease and introspection.

Winter Solstice

In the middle of the darkness, on the darkest night of the year, winter solstice shines forth as the turning point, the moment when the darkness no longer increases but begins to retreat. From this moment forward, light will increase as the days grow longer. The most potent energy of winter solstice is that promise of light to come. Indeed, there is no night so long it will not end, no dark so deep it will not brighten. With every lengthening day, we move closer to spring equinox. Thus, as the moon travels around the Earth, returning always to the beginning, so also does the Earth travel around the sun. To ancient peoples, however, it was the sun, moon, planets, and stars that circled the Earth, an error that led to one of the oldest and most sophisticated divination systems in the world—astrology.

Astrology

Many years ago, Isaac researched and wrote an article titled "Does Astrology Really Work?" (published in the now-defunct *Psychic Magazine*). In it he examined the two dozen or so scientific experiments that had been published up to that time that tested various astrological concepts. What he found was interesting on several levels. To begin with, many of the experiments had been done by people with only a cursory knowledge of astrology, and the results of these experiments tended to disprove the particular hypotheses being tested (that is, they had negative results). The experiments performed by people with an in-depth knowledge of astrology, however, tended to support their hypotheses (they had positive results). It's easy to assume that the experiments all ended in black and white, true or false results. Not so! About a third of them had negative results, a third had positive results, and the remaining third yielded results that did not match traditional astrological theories, but supported one of astrology's core concepts— namely, that birth time and place data could be used to predict personal characteristics and experiences.

Sir Isaac Newton (1643–1727), the pioneering physicist who gave the world its first laws of motion, famously once said to a fellow scientist who was criticizing him for believing in astrology, "I, sir, have studied the matter. You have not." Indeed, most criticism of astrology comes from people who have only the slightest knowledge of it (and usually the "sun sign astrology" of newspapers and magazines, a type of astrology that most professional astrologers look down upon themselves). The real thing is far more complex.

We both have "studied the matter," though not to the level of professionals. The following is our attempt to condense and summarize astrology in the simplest terms possible, temporarily putting aside the many complexities involved. There are two core concepts in astrology as it is practiced in the West.[3] The first is that the positions of the sun, moon, and planets of our solar system, as seen against the backdrop of the stars, have a subtle yet profound effect upon living things, including people. The second is that where and when a person is born determines much of how their life will unfold, because celestial positions place a kind of stamp on each newborn child.

The band of the sky through which the planets, sun, and moon (all of which are called planets or "wanderers" in astrology) move is what astronomers call the "ecliptic," or the plane on which most of the planets orbit the sun. Because many of the constellations are named after animals, this band is called by astrologers the "zodiac," or zoo. In ancient Babylon, where astrology originated, there were originally 10 "signs." We know these today by their Latin names: Aries the Ram, Taurus the Bull, Gemini the Twins, Cancer the Crab, Leo the Lion, Aquila the Eagle, Sagittarius the Archer, Capricorn the Goat, Aquarius the Water-bearer, and Pisces the Fish.

The Greeks left their mark on astrology by incorporating the four Elements, and by subdividing the Eagle sign into Virgo the Maiden, Libra the Scales, and Scorpio the Scorpion. This enabled Greek astrologers to construct a system of three "qualities" of signs for each of the Elements—cardinal, fixed, and mutable. Cardinal signs begin the seasons, and are thus associated with beginnings and people who are forward thinking. Fixed signs are at the height of their seasons, and are associated with strength and continuity, as well as those who are stubborn and tenacious. Mutable signs end their seasons and lead into the following ones, so they are associated with changes and mutability, and with those who are restless and adaptable.

As we already mentioned, the changes of the seasons can have profound effects upon people, through variations in temperature, hours of light and darkness, weather patterns, pollen counts, available foodstuffs, and so on. Perhaps the astrological qualities of the signs are based on observation as much as philosophy or metaphysics.

Element	Cardinal	Fixed	Mutable
Fire	Aries (spring)	Leo	Sagittarius
Water	Cancer (summer)	Scorpio	Pisces
Air	Libra (autumn)	Aquarius	Gemini
Earth	Capricorn (winter)	Taurus	Virgo

Table 2: *The astrological signs by Element and nature.*

Thus we can see that astrology is yet another mystical art wherein the distinctions between the physical, physiological, psychological, and metaphorical energies become almost completely blurred. Originally, the astrological planets were identified with various deities and credited with having mystical powers and influences appropriate to each such god or goddess, so that each planet was believed to "rule" over certain activities and characteristics,[4] as in this table:

Planet/Deity	Rulership
Sun (Sol)	Light, reason, glory
Moon (Selene)	Darkness, emotions, dreams
Mercury	Communication, tricks
Venus	Love, pleasure, beauty, womanliness
Mars	War, competition, manliness
Jupiter	Power, wealth, expansion
Saturn	Age, time, limitation
Uranus	Disruption, change, earthquakes
Neptune	Dreaminess, vagueness
Pluto	Death, finality

Table 3: *The astrological planets and their "rulerships."*

Ancient peoples didn't know about the outer planets, because they weren't visible to the naked eye, and so they didn't become part of astrology until the last two centuries. The seven visible planets gave us our names for the days of the week. Each was thought to be strengthened or weakened in its powers according to what zodiac sign it was seen in, and based on the sorts of geometric angles, or "aspects," it made to the other planets when drawn onto a horoscope (literally, "time observance") chart. Such charts were eventually drawn with 12 subdivisions called "houses," based on what part of the zodiac was rising on the eastern horizon at the time of a birth.

Ancient astronomer/astrologers (the two fields didn't part ways until a few hundred years ago) also worked with observations of how the "fixed" stars seemed to interact with the planets, and where these stars appeared in the houses of horoscope charts. Each astrological house, beginning with the ascendant, or rising sign, had its own zodiac sign, and was thought to be concerned with a different aspect of life, as shown in the following table:

Number/Name of House	Natural Sign	Concerns
First (Ascendant)	Aries	The self/ego, the body, beginnings
Second	Taurus	Values, resources, money
Third	Gemini	Short trips, siblings, childhood learning
Fourth (Immum Coeli)	Cancer	Home, old age, mothers
Fifth	Leo	Pleasure, lovers, children
Sixth	Virgo	Work, strength, pets
Seventh (Descendant)	Libra	Partners, others, enemies
Eighth	Scorpio	Sexuality, inheritance, death
Ninth	Sagittarius	Long trips, in-laws, higher learning
Tenth (Midheaven)	Capricorn	Status, the world, fathers
Eleventh	Aquarius	Goals, destiny, love
Twelfth	Pisces	Secrets, limits, problems

Table 4: *The astrological houses, with their attendant signs and concerns.*

A little thought will reveal that the concerns of each house match the Elemental attributions of each associated sign suspiciously well. So, even though astrologers insist that these correspondences are purely the result of centuries of observation, it seems clear to us that somebody somewhere put a lot of work into creating a system that would contain all the variables needed for a complex divination method, and yet be easy to memorize.

The geometric angles that can appear between planets, fixed stars, and house or sign cusps (points of transition) are called aspects. "Easy" aspects include conjunctions, where two or more seem very close; trines, where they make 60 degree angles to each other; and sextiles, where they make 30 degree angles. Negative or "difficult" aspects include oppositions of 180 degrees, squares of 90 degrees, and semisquares of 45 degrees. There are other aspects as well, based on all of the different ways that the full 360 degrees of a horoscope's circular chart can be divided.

Figure 14 on page 137 shows a typical, simplified horoscope, with the ascendant at 4 degrees of Aquarius, using the equal houses system (there are several ways to divide house cusps).

If we multiply 12 signs by 12 houses, we come up with a minimum of 144 different places that each of the 10 astrological planets can occupy in a horoscope. Multiple these possibilities by the dozen or so different kinds of aspects, and we have a huge number of possible outcomes. Can you see why scientific experiments based on only a handful of variables, and performed by people who may have widely differing levels of knowledge about astrology, can produce such divergent results?

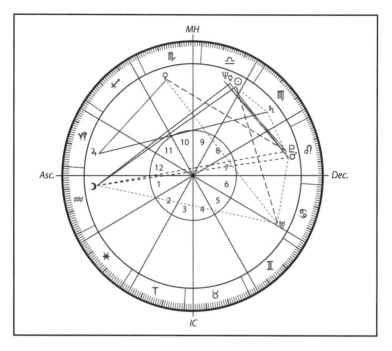

Figure 14: *A typical horoscope.*

Astrologers often talk about astrological energies, but what exactly do they mean? Well, it varies somewhat from one astrologer to another, but most seem to be signifying something that conflates several key ideas: the physical effects of the planets (for example, gravitation); the mathematical effects of the different aspects, which were originally based on numerology; the fact that the patterns in the chart taken as a whole seem to affect the astrologer or the person for whom it was cast psychologically; and how psychic the astrologer happens to be. Perhaps the primary purpose of a horoscope is to provide a magical or psychic link to the "native" (the person's whose birth, or "natal," chart is being read) through the magical laws of similarity and contagion.

Could there be actual physical effects on people from planetary positions? Gravity extends infinitely from its source of mass, but it's difficult to believe that the infinitesimally small gravitational influences of anything farther away than the moon could effect any noticeable change. The argument is often made by astrologers that, because the moon affects all bodies of water on Earth, and because humans are mostly water, there could be subtle interactions between human physiology and the movements of the moon's gravitational field as it orbits the Earth. Millennia of anecdotal evidence, as well as the statistical records of hospitals and police departments, show fluctuations of psychological disturbances and bleeding of wounds peaking at the full moon (which is why some hospitals—and wise patients—won't schedule elective surgery during that time). Whether this is caused by gravity or something else is unclear.

In 1974, a book titled *The Jupiter Effect* by John Gribbin looked at such statistical records, as well as records of earthquakes, and came to the incorrect conclusion that the gravity of the major planets and the moon could trigger earthquakes. The records also suggested that the gravitational influence of the major planets affect solar tides, which affect Earth's weather, which can have major effects on human and animal physiology and psychology. However, this is a far cry from claiming that the "Venusian energy" present at someone's birth influenced him or her to become an artist or, if badly aspected, a prostitute. There is, after all, absolutely nothing about the planet Venus that is in the least bit loving, pleasant, or creative—it's an infernal stewpot of boiling sulfuric acid clouds! It is beautiful in the night sky, however, and that says to us that its metaphorical powers may be far more important than any quasi-physical energies it may be sending in our direction. We've certainly noticed over the years that the efficacy of planetary energies in magic seems to depend more on the consciousness of the magician and her or his associational systems, than on anything absolute. This applies to the use of Elemental energies as well.

So is astrology an art or a science? Most modern astrologers will say that it is both. Personally, we've seen enough examples of purely mechanical interpretations of horoscope charts done by computers that yielded dead-on accurate results (far beyond what can be explained away as coincidence or selective attention) that we are inclined to think there is some sort of science involved, albeit a "soft" one. Yet we've also seen a chart passed around to different astrologers, each of whom had slightly different interpretations that brought out different ideas and information about the person for whom the chart was cast, some with high and some with low accuracy. As with so many other topics we are covering in this book, our conclusions here will just have to be ambiguous.

Earth Energies and Ley Lines

When we move our attention from the heavens over our heads to the ground beneath our feet, we discover yet another category of mystical energies embraced and used by mystics, magicians, New Agers, and Neo-Pagans alike: Earth energies. Most of these are discussed in other chapters of this book. To some people this term refers to the various energies, spiritual and otherwise, of Gaia—the personification of the Earth's biosphere, or the mystic energies of the world of the land, including its plants and animals. To others, Earth energies are the same as the Elemental Earth energies discussed in Chapter 3. Those who use crystals, minerals, jewels, and other rocks to generate or store mystical forces sometimes refer to all these items as having Earth energies.

Perhaps the Earth energies best known to most New Agers and modern metaphysicians are the ones that supposedly flow or run through the surface of the Earth along what are usually called ley lines. These lines, which may or may not be similar to the Chinese dragon lines, are said to connect many ancient monuments and megalithic (literally, "big stone") constructions, and can often be traced across hundreds or even thousands of miles. Although there are a wide variety of theories regarding these lines, skeptical archeologists and anthropologists have noted the common human tendency to connect buildings with straight lines, as it provides the shortest path to travel between them.

Some lines point to astronomical event locations, such as the line that runs from the center of Stonehenge, through the two heel stones originally outside of the circle,[5] and off to the horizon where the summer solstice sunrise occurs. A number of such alignments, often passing through major megalithic sites, have been discovered by archeologists, and astronomical explanations for their existence are often considered plausible by astronomers. However, astronomical alignments are not necessarily the same thing as ley lines.

It's also possible that some ley lines are simply the result of modern people drawing lines on maps, then looking for buildings, standing stones, monuments, or other important sites on or near the lines, no matter how widely separated these sites are by century of origin. Skeptics and cynics have claimed that all ley lines are the result of pure chance; given a large enough sample of locations, some straight lines will be sure to connect several of them.

True believers in the mystical powers of ley lines, such as the many fans of John F. Michell's *The New View Over Atlantis*, insist that the natural electrical currents in the Earth's crust (called "telluric currents"), other magnetic currents in the Earth, and underground streams of water all flow along ley lines. Dowsers ("water witches") are frequently employed by farmers and engineering firms to trace such currents and flows. Some people believe that mystical energies travel along, and can be tapped from, these natural kinds of energy flow. Some also believe that ancient peoples knew about these mystical energies, and built their important cultural monuments at intersection points of the ley lines accordingly.

The idea that these energies can be tapped is not wholly unreasonable. Many years ago, Isaac learned that he could tap or draw out psychical, magical, or mystical energy from light fixtures and wall switches (though it tended to shorten the working life of the fixtures). He first attempted this after having noticed how he could tap such energy from the air during thunderstorms, though that probably involved several other factors besides the electrical and magnetic fields. He suggested, half seriously, that there were "electrical Elementals" he called "ergs,"[6] and worked with them for several weeks until he and his roommate noticed their electric bills going sky high and had to cease their experiments. And speaking of experiments: because many people believe that long-range telepathy is easier to do if the participants are on a ley line, it would be well worth the time and energy(!) to see just how well this really works. For now, however, let's discuss a somewhat related exercise done in many Western esoteric movements, something known as "grounding and centering." What does this phrase really mean?

Grounding and Centering?

"Okay, everyone, ground and center!"

What's with the blank look? You mean, you're familiar with the phrase (whether spoken or written) but you don't have a clue as to what you are actually supposed to do? Here's the good news: you're not alone. A lot of otherwise knowledgeable and experienced people (but never your esteemed authors) will blithely assume that everyone knows exactly what they mean by the phrase. After all, it's a basic exercise. It's the starting point for just about every ritual, so everyone knows what it is and how to do it, right? And, of course, you're not about to raise your hand and ask, "Please explain," because, well, it's so obvious that everyone else knows what it means and how to do it.[7] As it is the starting point for so many energy exercises, let's make sure we're all on the same page, so to speak. Here's how it's supposed to work:

Though often linked together in practice, grounding and centering your mystical energies are two separate processes. Let's start by defining each one. "Grounding" is one of those energy words taken from technology—in this case, electricity. To an electrician, to ground (or "earth") a current is to direct it into the ground, where it can then dissipate harmlessly. The earth can absorb and dissipate a great amount of electrical energy. Thus, electrical wiring is typically grounded so that a short circuit (a flow of electricity heading somewhere where it's not supposed to go) will be redirected harmlessly into the earth. Lighting rods work the same way: Lighting is attracted to the metallic rod more easily than to the structure to which it is attached, and any lightning strike will flow through a wire attached to the rod and into the earth. When many energy workers use the word grounding, they mean more or less the same thing—taking excess energy or energy that is heading somewhere it isn't supposed to go and diverting it into the earth.

A secondary usage of the term, when it is most often coupled with "centering," refers to the drawing up of energy from the earth (the ground) and into the practitioner. The Earth is a vast reservoir of energy (all that lightning has to go somewhere, we suppose), both physical and mystical, the latter of which is considered to be stable and strong. Both methods of grounding can have the effect of putting your mystical energy into neutral. In the first case, you are getting rid of excess energy; in the second instance you are replenishing lost or depleted energy.

Centering is a function of attention. All energy-working systems seem to agree that *energy follows attention*. Whether you're pointing your finger or focusing on your breath, your energy will follow. Centering, therefore, is moving your attention inside yourself, to your center. This shift of attention creates what could be thought of as an energy "center of gravity" inside yourself. In physics, the center of gravity or center of mass is the point where a body acts as if its mass is concentrated. This center is not necessarily the geometric center or middle of an object. For example, if you wish to change the center of gravity of a car, you don't need to change the shape of the car; you can add weight, or merely shift some of its weight to the bottom of the vehicle. This will lower the car's center of gravity and change the way it is balanced. Thus, it becomes easier to steer on curves and less likely to roll over.

When you center yourself, you are shifting energy to create a stable center of balance within yourself. Why would this be important? To paraphrase the bodywork pioneer Moshe Feldenkrais (1904–1984), from a state of balance we can move freely in any direction. It's similar to having your weight evenly balanced on both feet. If you want to lift one foot or the other, or if you want to go left, right, or back and forth, you can do so freely. But what if you are standing with your weight shifted over your right leg? You can move freely in some directions, but not all. If Simon said to wiggle your right foot, you would first have to shift your weight to the left leg. That's not such a big deal in a game, but if you're in a chorus line, that might leave you a step behind everyone else. Or, if you're a martial artist, it might get you a kick in the head.

People who work with their bodies, such as dancers, martial artists, and gymnasts, are constantly moving through that point of balance and then back to it so they can be ready for the next move. The point of centering your mystical energy is much the same. You are creating a focused, balanced state within yourself from which you can then move freely. You are ready, energetically, for whatever comes next, whether it be ritual, healing, meditation, or even the SATs.

Exercise 3:

Grounding and Centering Your Mystical Energies

Grounding (in both senses) and centering, while reasonably distinct activities on their own, are in practice usually inextricably linked together. Use the following techniques to bring your personal energy to a state of balance before you begin the next stage of your work. Depending on the point from which you are starting, you may emphasize any one method over another.

Most techniques for grounding and centering employ some form of visualization. In group situations, a facilitator may lead the group through guided visual imagery, often incorrectly called guided meditation, so that the entire group can start off on the same wavelength (so to speak). Review our general instructions regarding exercises from the Introduction. If you've read the Pre-Exercise Exercise in Chapter 2, you already know how to create an environment and access a body state that will help you focus. Use that as a starting place for this exercise.

Settle yourself into a comfortable, upright position. Uncross your legs, take your hands out of your pockets, and shake your fingers loose. If you are standing, place your feet about shoulder-width apart, and allow your arms to hang loosely at your side. Rock back and forth, heel to toe, briefly, until your weight feels balanced evenly over your feet. If you are seated, place your feet flat on the floor, with your arms lying loosely on your lap and your hands open and unclasped. Hold your head erect (your back will follow).

Now, do an energy assessment of yourself. (At this point you may find it helpful to close your eyes.) Do you feel calm, excited, nervous, relaxed, tense? Is your knee bouncing? Is it difficult to stand still? Are you close to falling asleep? Is it difficult to turn the page? You do not need to change or judge anything— just notice yourself. If you notice that you feel charged up, the exercise will help drain off excess energy. If you notice that you feel depleted, the exercise will help replenish your energy. You have already begun to make this assessment by turning your attention inward.

Take the following steps:

✦ Take three deep breaths.

✦ With each breath, relax into your standing or sitting position.

- ✦ Take three more deep breaths.

- ✦ As you inhale, seek out any tension in your body. As you exhale, send the tension out with your breath.

- ✦ Take another deep breath, letting the breath drift down from your lungs and settle in your feet.

- ✦ Breathe again.

- ✦ Let your breath and your awareness settle in the soles of your feet. Notice the feel of your socks or shoes, or your bare feet on the floor or the ground.

- ✦ Breathe again.

- ✦ As you inhale, send roots of awareness out of the bottoms of your feet.

- ✦ With each breath, send the roots further down.

Now, adapt the following narrative to your environment and circumstances:

Send your roots down through your socks, through your shoes, through the carpet, through the floor, through the ceiling below, and down through the room below that. Push through the floor, the basement, and the foundation. Send your roots down and down, through the dirt, through the gravel, through the groundwater; send them into the bedrock, finding every crack and fissure, pushing down, down into the Earth. Down and down, until the rocks themselves get warmer and warmer; through the crust, through the mantle, down to the core and the liquid rocks, down and down to the very center, until your roots touch on the heart of the planet.

Let your roots wrap around the core. Feel the power of the heart of the Earth.

Breathe deeply.

As you inhale, pull the Earth energy up through your roots. Let it flow up toward you, past the liquid rock, past the hot rock, through the bedrock, up and up, through the ground water, through the gravel, through the dirt; up and up with every breath, let it flow through your roots past the foundation, through the floor, up to your feet, into your feet.

Feel the connection to the center of the Earth.

Breathe deeply.

With every breath, pull more of the Earth's energy into your feet. Let it flow upward into your ankles, into your calves, into your thighs, into your pelvis. Send the energy into your belly, into your torso, into your lungs and heart; down your shoulders into your arms, into your hands; up your shoulders into your neck, into your head.

Breathe again.

Feel the Earth energy all through your body.

Let the Earth energy flow out of your head, your arms, and your shoulders like tiny branches that grow larger and larger. Let your branches burst forth with buds and leaves as they reach for the sky, the sunlight, and the stars beyond. Draw the nourishment of the sun and stars back through your leaves and through your branches, back into your body, down and around, until it mixes and blends with the Earth energy within you.

Now you're grounded and centered!

Chapter 5

Chinese Esoteric Energies

The tao that can be told
is not the eternal Tao.
The name that can be named
is not the eternal Name.
The unnamable is the eternally real.
Naming is the origin
of all particular things.
Free from desire, you realize the mystery.
Caught in desire, you see only the
manifestations.
Yet mystery and manifestations
arise from the same source.
This source is called darkness.
Darkness within darkness.
The gateway to all understanding.[1]

—Lao-tzu (c. 551–479 B.C.E.)

The Tao, Yin, and Yang

There are few things more humbling than researching a topic only to find that what you thought you knew about it was, well, not quite right (okay, kinda wrong). That's where we found ourselves with Taoism. Previously we'd gone with the flow of the casual use of the word Tao (properly pronounced "dow"). For most folks in the Western world, flow is what the Tao is all about. Go with the flow. Be one with the Tao. Get yourself in the zone. Be one with what you're doing. Very Zen.

However, as often happens with an Eastern idea that has migrated to Western brains, this New Age idea of the Tao has drifted pretty far from its roots. While flow and harmony are certainly part of Chinese Taoism, the real thing is far more sophisticated and complex. Tao is a religion, a philosophy, and a way of life, with roots going back more than 25 centuries. Going with the flow is but a small part of this—and "Zen" isn't part of it at all. It is far beyond the scope of this book to give a complete picture of Taoism, so we're going to limit ourselves to the simplest uses of the term, as it is most commonly found in energy work. After all, to quote Lao-tzu, "The Tao that can be told is not the eternal Tao" (from the *Tao Te Ching*, attributed to the legendary Chinese philosopher Lao-tzu, and traditionally dated to 500 B.C.E.). It is from this slim book—really a collection of verses, Chinese wisdom sayings, and Taoist teachings, likely compiled about 200 years later—that most Westerners have gotten their ideas about the Tao and Taoism.

Tao and Taoism

What is the Tao? It isn't a thing. You can't touch the Tao or put it in a box, but at the same time, it's not "nothing," either. The Tao is everything: It is the underlying principle of the world, and the natural order of the universe—which, by the way, is ultimately good. An approximate translation of Tao would be "road" or "way." Thus, the Tao is both the world and a way of being in the world. When you are on the road, "with" the road, and traveling down the road all at the same time ("tao" can be a noun or a verb), you are in harmony with the world and its flow of events. This goes for complex systems such as governments, too.

While roads can lead you in various directions, water flows in only one direction at a time. Thus water is a major metaphor for Taoism. Flowing water has a current upon which a leaf can flow effortlessly. Flowing water will eventually wear down all obstacles—not through force, but simply by being itself. Water not allowed to flow will become stagnant and nasty.

How do you know when you're one with the flow? Life gets easier, and better. One discovers the Tao through simplicity, spontaneity, and meditation. Contemplation of nature will reveal the Tao much better than any rigid constructs of society (which reveals one of the roots of Taoism's inception as a reaction against the rule-bound rigidity of Confucianism). The iconic image of Taoism is the yin-yang symbol, also called the *taiji* or *taijitu*.

Yin and yang are the interconnected opposites—the light and the dark, the everything and the nothing, both connected to and containing the other. The universe is the flow and flux between these poles, with the interplay of their forces creating all that is. Everything is "either" yin or yang. We put "either" in quotes because yin and yang, while opposites, are not dualistic. In dualism, something that is not one thing must, by definition, be the other. If it's light, it's not dark. If it's day, it's not night. If it's bad, it's not good—not no way, not no how.

Figure 15: *The yin-yang symbol.*

As we discussed previously, this kind of dualistic thinking leaves out all sorts of shades of grey and "twilight" areas, including, well, actual twilight for one, or things that may be good in one context but bad in another. It's good (albeit dangerous) to drive 150 miles per hour in a NASCAR race, but not so good (and really dangerous) to do the same thing on a residential street. Same energy, different application!

The yin-yang symbol expresses the philosophy of Taoism by showing a dot of each principle in the body of the other. Part of yin is within yang, and part of yang is within yin. Everything contains its opposite, and nothing is complete without its "other." Thus, every person, every thing, and every situation is a blend of yin and yang. The universe itself is self-correcting in this regard: when flow goes too far in any one direction, it turns back upon itself, just as in the illustration, always seeking to achieve balance and harmony.

In broad terms, yin expresses the dark, yielding, internal energies, while yang expresses the bright, indomitable, external energies. (Need we repeat these are not absolutes?) Yin energy is also female, while yang is male. Although these are definitive distinctions in the Chinese idea of yin-yang, the suggestion of assigning any qualities to gender is so loaded a topic in today's society that we almost hesitate to include it!

Here is a table showing some typical yin-yang attributions, taken from multiple sources and our own personal experiences:

Yin	Yang	Yin	Yang
feminine	masculine	winter	summer
mothers	fathers	interior	surface
daughters	sons	blood	skin
receptive	projective	intangible	tangible
too little	too much	intuitive	rational
internal	external	stillness	activity
dark	light	resting	working
moon	sun	sleep	wakefulness
night	day	feeling	thinking
cold	hot	philosophy	mathematics
moist	dry	sociology	physics

Table 5: *Some examples of yin and yang.*

The idea of energy flux, flow, and balance, as it is expressed in the Tao and illustrated in the yin-yang symbol, is critical to understanding systems such as feng shui, acupuncture, and other forms of oriental medicine, and even the martial arts.

Qi Concepts

Qi (also *ch'i* or *chi*, or *ki* in Japanese, is the fundamental energy flow of the universe, the life force or underlying and unifying energy of, well, everything. People have qi. Places have qi. Qi is what the acupuncturist pokes at, and what you're balancing when you feng shui your house. Qi is the ch'i in t'ai chi and the ki in akido. Qi is what you're revving up with the karate yell right before you break that board. Qi is the breath and the energy you're developing in the practice of qi gong. In fact, qi is often translated as "life's breath," or "cosmic breath." Chinese "astrology" is based in part upon the qi you inhaled with your first breath.

Qi has been a fundamental part of Chinese culture and thinking for thousands of years. As is typical with representations of things that are as much metaphysical as they are physical, definitions and descriptions of qi have varied widely over the millennia. For example, when discussing the relationship between matter and qi, some say matter came from qi, some say qi came from matter, some say qi and matter are the same thing, and some say matter is an illusion, so it's really a moot point.

There are three major kinds of qi, which could be referred to as cosmic or celestial qi, human or animal qi, and earthly or terrestrial qi. The first kind comes from the sun, moon, planets, and stars, as well as the weather. The second kind is what flows through people and animals, and is crystallized at birth when a baby takes his or her first breath. The third kind is the qi of mountains, rivers, lakes, deserts, forests, and so on. Qi in a general sense can be seen as the Chinese version of the life force or orgone energy we discussed previously, as well as a quantum field connecting everything in the universe. Whether it is both things or not remains to be determined—maybe the Tao is the quantum field of qi!

So what's the key to understanding qi? It's not so different from our description of the Tao. When everything is going with the Tao, the qi is flowing in the right direction and with the correct balance. When qi is out of balance, too intense, too weak, or just plain "stuck," that's when things go awry. Qi flow is also a critical concept in acupuncture, the traditional Chinese healing modality, which we will discuss in Chapter 8.

Qi gong, pronounced "chee gung," is a system of physical and mental exercises designed to improve the quality of one's internal qi flows, and thus promote healing, strength, and stamina. *Wei dan* refers to the actual physical exercises, and *nei dan* to the mental ones. Careful breathing is important in all of these exercises. Because *qi* means "air" or "energy," and *gong* means "work," qi gong becomes "breath work" or "energy work." There are thousands of qi gong exercises that have been invented over the last 2,500-plus years, most of them focused on removing qi blocks and improving qi flow by relaxing the mind, body, and emotions.

Qi gong practices are categorized as *dong gong* (active or yang) or *jing gong* (passive or yin). The former includes physical exercises such t'ai chi, while the latter involves quiet sitting or standing, and breathing and visualization techniques designed to focus attention on the body. To quote David W. Sollars, "Qi

Gong is...about realizing that the body isn't a solid entity, but instead an open moving wave of energy. Qi Gong will actually help you realize your energy nature by providing quiet sitting exercises that enable you to feel it."[2]

Five Elements—But Different?

The so-called five Elements attributed to the Chinese really have nothing to do with our Western Elemental system. As we discussed previously, you could look upon the four Elements— Air, Earth, Fire, and Water—as the essential pieces or building blocks of everything else. However, the Chinese five Elements— Fire, Earth, Metal, Water, and Wood—are considered *phases* through which energy (qi) passes as it moves through the cycle of yin and yang.

The simplest way to understand these phases are as movements. The movement of rising energy would be represented by Fire, while falling energy is represented by Water. Likewise, Earth qi is revolving, Metal qi contracting, and Wood qi expanding. Just as the Western Elements have their correspondences, the five phases have their own attributes as well. Body parts, seasons, and directions, and qualities such as cold, heat, wetness, or dryness, can all be categorized according to phase.

This may seem simple enough—except it's actually a tad more complicated. Right off the bat, you've got four seasons and five phases. Add in three cycles, eight cardinal directions (with 24 "distinctions"), 28 constellations, eight trigrams, the nine numbers of Luoshu's magic square, divide it all by five, and you've got a word problem (in Chinese, no less) of epic proportions. This is why people spend entire lifetimes studying Chinese concepts of esoteric energies, and die feeling that they have only scratched the surface.

Feng Shui

Forget about the little mirrors, hanging flutes, electric water fountains, and all the other cute tchotchkes that have become associated with feng shui since 1980 or so. True feng shui (literally, "wind and water," and pronounced "fung shway"), is an incredibly complex Chinese system for restoring harmonious energy through an understanding of qi and its phases. Authentic feng shui practitioners scoff at what most of us think we know about the art. Little mirrors don't reflect qi back at you, nor does leaving the toilet lid open flush your luck away. Serious feng shui looks not just at your decor, but at the placement of your building, your date of birth, your building's date of birth, compass alignments, and nearby natural and manmade features.

The form school of feng shui is probably the original system. It was used to orient tombs so that ancestors would feel comfortable and thus beneficent toward their descendents. The form school is a more intuitive, yin way of choosing appropriate locations and décor, based on such things as the shape of the land and the presence of water or wind. The compass school of feng shui is a more intellectual, yang approach. It is dependent on calculations involving eight directions, each with three distinctions that are associated with different qualities of qi, and modified by the notable presence or absence of each of the five Elements.

In a given location, qi may be *sheng qi* (positive or auspicious) or *sha qi* (negative or inauspicious). Sheng qi comes with things that delight the senses, whereas sha qi comes with things that antagonize them, as shown in Table 6 on page 158.

Sense	Sheng Qi	Sha Qi
Vision	Beautiful and happy sights	Ugly, nasty, glaring, distasteful sights
Hearing	Happy, cheerful, soothing sounds; quiet and stillness	Unpleasant sounds, racket
Touch	Things that are pleasing to touch; touches that are pleasing	Dirt, filth, unpleasant surfaces; unwelcome contact
Smell	Pleasant scents	Rot, pollution
Taste	Rich and enjoyable foods and beverages	Spoiled food, toxins
Psychic	Intuitions of positive events, love, confidence, contentment; the presence of helpful and kind people or spirits.	Intuitions of negative events, hate, worry, tension; the presence of hostile people or spirits.

Table 6: *Positive and negative qi.*

Then there's the matter of the three cycles of the five Elements or phases of qi. Each flows into and out of the others in three main ways, as shown in Table 7 on page 159.

The eight trigrams, which are the root of the 64 hexagrams of the *I Ching*, are composed of all the possible combinations of three yin (broken) and/or three yang (solid) lines or bars. Each of the trigrams has multiple concepts associated with it, in a system as complex as anything a Western Cabalist ever dreamed. The eight trigrams taken together represent the energy of all

Cycle	Productive or Generating	Dominant or Controlling	Destructive or Reductive
Process	Each Element generates the next (mother/child)	Each Element controls, checks, and regulates others (father/child)	An Element becomes excessive, causing another one to become deficient
Changes	Fire leaves ashes which become Earth, which is the nest for Metal, whose contraction produces Water, which is essential to the growth of Wood, which dries and goes back to Fire	Fire melts Metal, which pierces Wood, which burdens Earth, which blocks Water, which diminishes Fire	Fire burns Wood, which absorbs Water, which corrodes Metal, which moves Earth, which reduces Fire

Table 7: *The three cycles of the five phases of qi ("Elements").*

possible situations. Each trigram can have a number assigned to it as well; these numbers are placed around the edges of a chart with nine squares called "Luoshu's magic square," with an empty cell in the middle. This arrangement is used by feng shui practitioners to calculate the attributes of a building. In the example shown in Figure 16 on page 160, notice how the numbers add up to 15 in any direction.

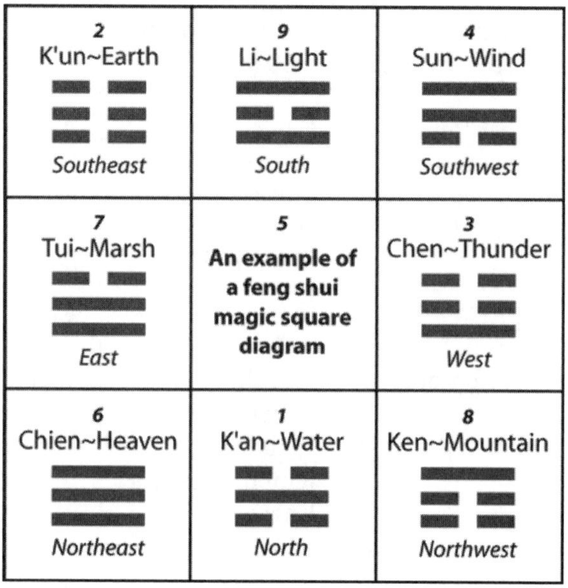

2 K'un~Earth Southeast	9 Li~Light South	4 Sun~Wind Southwest
7 Tui~Marsh East	5 An example of a feng shui magic square diagram	3 Chen~Thunder West
6 Chien~Heaven Northeast	1 K'an~Water North	8 Ken~Mountain Northwest

Figure 16: *A feng shui "magic" square.*

The goal of a feng shui practitioner is to help people locate, rearrange, or remodel their living or working quarters so that the different kinds of external qi (both celestial and terrestrial) will flow through a building harmoniously, thus positively affecting the internal qi of the people living or working there.

Chinese "Astrology"

The process of applying the principles of Taoism and feng shui to humans is what Westerners call Chinese astrology, though it bears little or no similarity to any other form of astrology. Most of us are familiar with the animals on the placemats at some Chinese restaurants. If you know the year in which you were born (don't laugh—Grandpa Heyman wasn't sure if he was 89 or 91), you can determine if you are a Rabbit, a Pig, a Horse, or one of the other featured creatures of the Chinese Zodiac. Unlike the Zodiac beloved by newspaper astrologers everywhere, this one does not relate these critters to constellations overhead. There might be a Scorpio in the stars, but there is nary a Monkey to be seen.

Chinese astrology is really an analysis of the qi that affects your life. Your birth-year sign represents the qi you inhaled at the moment of your first breath. By refining your knowledge of the branches and phases of qi at the precise month, day, and even hour of your birth, you will gain a more complete understanding of your life, your fate, and your compatibilities with others.

Each year, or more precisely, each solar cycle that begins at the midpoint between winter solstice and spring equinox (the Chinese New Year), is assigned an animal. The particular characteristics of each animal represent a certain type of Earth qi that is present during that particular cycle of time. While we are most familiar with the repeating cycle of 12 animals over 12 years, our cosmic critters are also assigned to repeating cycles of 12 months, and 12 two-hour increments. These divisions are called the Twelve Earthly Branches, and represent qi at a place in space. Thus, you could be a Rabbit born in a Monkey month at an Ox hour.

In addition, the qi of the Twelve Earthly Branches passes through the five phases of Fire, Earth, Metal, Water and Wood, which are further categorized as either yin or yang. These five phases times two polarizations are called the Ten Heavenly Stems (or the Ten Stems of Time), and they chart the movement of qi through time and the seasons. It takes a full 60 years for the planetary and cosmic qi to run through all the permutations of phases and animals. Thus, you could have yin fire Snake qi (at least, we think you could) and not encounter a younger version of yourself before the generation of your grandchildren or great grandchildren.

This is just the start of a serious analysis of your birth qi. The exact details are calculated using the Four Pillars of Destiny. Each component of the moment of your birth, the hour, day, month, and year, has its own pillar. Each pillar is then composed of four components, reflecting the correlation of that hour, day, and year to 1) one each of the Ten Heavenly Stems and Twelve Earthly Branches, and 2) the appropriate phase of that stem and branch.

But wait, there's more. Now you can look at the 16 components of your Four Pillars, pinpoint your day-master phase, and work out which of five possible qi conditions—timely, weak, locked, dead, or ready, depending upon the literal season of the year into which you were born—apply to the day-master. You can figure out how the other seven phases apply to the day-master, and then work out the relationships based on five interpretive phases: resource, intelligence, power, wealth, and parallel.

All that from that one first deep breath. Whew!

So all that stuff we thought we knew about Chinese mysticism? That was Zen; this is Tao.

Exercise 4:
Making a Ball of Qi

This may actually be the oldest exercise in the book. It's central to the practice of t'ai chi, and variations of it can be found in all energy systems. Here's our version.

Creating the Energy Ball

Stand or sit upright with your feet planted squarely on the floor. Ground and center yourself as described in Exercise 3.

You should be relaxed but alert. Rub your hands together vigorously. Move them apart about an inch or so. You will feel a tingly sensation, as if there is something tangible floating between your hands. There is something tangible there: energy. We'll leave speculation on just what that energy is, or where it comes from, to other parts of this book. Right now, what you're feeling is the energy that will make the energy ball.

Slowly move your hands farther apart. How far apart can you move them and still feel the tingle? Go back and forth until you have a sense of the energy field's outer limits. Now cup your hands slightly as if you were forming a snowball or wrapping your hands around a grapefruit. As the position of your hands changes, feel the energy roll into a ball shape. Roll it around in your hands. Feel what happens as you bring your hands closer together and farther apart. Add more energy to the ball. Let energy flow through you and out your hands into the ball. Continue rolling the ball around in your hands. Enlarge it by moving your hands farther apart. Make it larger and larger, as if you were holding a beach ball that was slowly inflating.

Energy Ball Games

Roll the ball up and down your body. Hold the ball in front of you, over your head, and behind you. What happens if you try to pass it through your body? Dance with the ball, as rhythmic gymnasts do. Play games with the ball. Can you toss it from hand to hand? Can you bounce and catch it? Can you hand it to another person? Can you merge your ball with someone else's? What happens if you drop it? Practice making it smaller and larger, weaker and stronger, by changing the position of your hands and manipulating the energy flow into the ball.

Chapter 6

Rocks, Plants, and Animals

Exercise 5:

Sensing Energy in Crystals and Other Objects

In a comfortable, quiet place, lay out several different types of stones and crystals. Ground and center yourself, as in Exercise 3. Take up each stone, one by one, and hold it between the palms of your hands.

Close your eyes.

Note any impressions, however slight or fuzzy, you get from the stone. Take whatever time you need. Let your imagination roam. Does it feel dull or tingly? Does it suggest a story? When you have held each stone, compare your impressions of them. Does one feel colder or warmer than the others? Do some tingle and others not? Do you prefer the feel of one stone over another?

Now close your eyes and mix up the stones. Pick them up again, one by one, and see if you can tell the individual stones apart by the way their energies feel to you. To take it a step further, let a friend choose a selection of crystals that have been charged for different purposes. See if you can pick out which one is which, based on energy feel alone.

Did you feel nothing at all? Well, maybe rocks aren't your thing. Try the same method with twigs from different trees, kitchen herbs and spices, feathers from a bird you don't know the species of, or fur from an animal you don't know.

Crystals, Minerals, and Gems

Francis Barrett, in Chapter 8 of *The Magus*, gives a classic presentation of what he calls "the Wonderful Virtues of Some Kinds of Precious Stones":

> It is a common opinion of magicians, that stones inherit great virtues, which they receive through the spheres and activity of the celestial influences, by the medium of the soul or spirit of the world. Authors very much disagree in respect of the probability of their actually having such virtues in potentia, some debating warmly against any occult or secret virtue lying hid in them; others, as warmly, showing the causes and effects of these sympathetic properties.
>
> However, to leave these trifling arguments to those who love cavil and contentions better than I do, and, as I have neither leisure nor inclination to enter the lists with sophists, and tongue-philosophers; I say, that these occult virtues are disposed throughout the animal, vegetable, and mineral kingdoms, by seeds, or ideas originally emanating from the Divine mind, and through super-celestial spirits and intelligence always operating, according to their proper offices and governments allotted them; which virtues are infused, as we before said,

through the medium of the Universal Spirit, as by a general and manifest sympathy and antipathy established in the law of Nature.

Amongst a variety of examples, the loadstone is one most remarkable proof of the sympathy and antipathy we speak of. However to hasten to the point. Amongst stones, those which resemble the rays of the sun by their golden sparklings, (as does the glittering stone ætites) prevent the falling-sickness [epilepsy] and poisons, if worn on the finger; so the stone which is called oculis solis, or eye of the sun, being in figure like to the apple of the eye, from which shines forth a ray, comforts the brain, and strengthens sight; the carbuncle, which shines by night, hath a virtue against all airy and vaporous poisons; the chrysolite stone, of a light green colour, when held against the sun, there shines in it a ray like a star of gold; this is singularly good for the lungs, and cures asthmatical complaints [asthma]; and if it be bored through, and the hollow filled with the mane of an ass, and bound to the left arm, it chases away all foolish and idle imaginations and melancholy fears, and drives away folly.[1]

The stone called iris, which is like crystal in colour, being found with six corners, when held in the shade, and the sun suffered to shine through it, represents a natural rainbow in the air. The stone heliotropium, green, like a jasper or emerald, beset with red specks, makes the wearer constant, renowned, and famous, and conduces to long life; there is, likewise, another wonderful property in this stone, and that is, that it so dazzles the eyes of men, that it causes the bearer to be invisible;

but then there must be applied to it the herb bearing the same name, viz. heliotropium, or the sun-flower; and these kind of virtues Albertus Magnus, and William of Paris, mention in their writings.

The jacinth also possesses virtue from the sun against poisons, pestilences, and pestiferous vapours; likewise it renders the bearer pleasant and acceptable; conduces, also, to gain money; being simply held in the mouth, it wonderfully cheers the heart, and strengthens the mind. Then there is the pyrophilus, of a red mixture, which Albertus Magnus reports that Æsculapius makes mention of in one of his epistles to Octavius Cæsar, saying, "There is a certain poison, so intensely cold, which preserves the heart of man, being taken out, from burning; so that if it be put into the fire for any time, it is turned into a stone, which stone is called pyrophilus:" it possesses a wonderful virtue against poison; and it infallibly renders the wearer thereof renowned and dreadful to his enemies. Apollonius is reported to have found a stone called pantaura, (which will attract other stones, as the loadstone does iron) most powerful against all poisons: it is spotted like the panther, and therefore some naturalists have given this stone the name of pantherus: Aaron calls it evanthum; and some, on account of its variety, call it pantochras.[2]

At the risk of being considered people "who love cavil and contentions" more than our distinguished predecessor—or, worse yet, as "sophists and tongue-philosophers"—we feel the need to point out some core concepts exemplified in Barrett's famous text. One of the purposes of this book is to examine whether certain traditional beliefs regarding mystical energies—for example, that they are inherent in certain objects, such as rocks—can be backed up by any known scientific knowledge, or if they are the artificial creations of metaphysicians and mystics at best, or just superstition at worst. Few other areas of mystical discussion offer as many opportunities for this kind of debate as that of crystals, minerals, and gems. Even the most modern New Age treatises on the topic contain many of these ancient ideas, namely:

✦ That some rocks have special virtues or powers because of astrological, planetary effects ("the spheres and activity of the celestial influences"). This is a purely natural explanation by modern New Age standards.

✦ That these planetary effects find purchase in the medium of Earth's mystical energy field or fields ("the soul or spirit of the world"), and/or the quantum field or God[3] (the "Universal Spirit"). This is a metaphysical and mystical explanation.

✦ That these virtues also are God's ideas or seeds distributed by angelic ("super-celestial"—beyond even the planets and stars) spirits. This is a purely religious explanation.

✦ That these virtues are based in positive and negative energy currents or fields ("a general and manifest sympathy and antipathy"), as exemplified by lodestones—magnetized rocks that have positive and negative poles. This is another natural New Age explanation.

Other than the lodestone and the one kind of crystal that works as a prism, almost all of the special rocks mentioned by Barrett are examples of the magical laws of similarity and association in action. Each rock has a physical resemblance to, or an astrological planetary association with, a given goal, so it can then magically or mystically produce that desired result. This is very similar to the doctrine of signatures in herbalism, in that such powers are considered to be inherent in each variety of rock, rather than something that has to be intentionally imbued into a stone by a magician, priest, or mystic. (In other words, God or the universe already did that for us.)

Manly Palmer Hall, in his magnum opus, *The Secret Teachings of All Ages*, writes:

Mythology abounds with accounts of magical rings and talismanic jewels. In the second book of his Republic, Plato describes a ring which, when the collet[4] was turned inward, rendered its wearer invisible. With this Gyges, the shepherd, secured for himself the throne of Lydia. Josephus also describes magical rings designed by Moses and King Solomon, and Aristotle mentions one which brought love and honor to its possessor. In his chapter dealing with the subject, Henry Cornelius Agrippa not only mentions the same rings, but states, upon the authority of Philostratus Jarchus, that Apollonius of Tyana extended his life to over 20 years with the aid of seven magical rings presented to him by an East Indian prince. Each of these seven rings was set with a gem partaking of the nature of one of the seven ruling planets of the week, and by daily changing the rings Apollonius protected himself against sickness and death by the intervention of the planetary influences. The philosopher also instructed his disciples in the virtues of these talismanic jewels, considering such information to be indispensable to the theurgist.[5] Agrippa describes the preparation of magical rings as follows: 'When any Star [planet] ascends fortunately, with the fortunate aspect or conjunction of the Moon, we must take a stone and herb that is under that Star, and make a ring of the metal that is suitable to this Star, and in it fasten the stone, putting the herb or root under it—not omitting the inscriptions of images, names, and characters, as also the proper suffumigations [burning of incense]." In describing the regalia of a [a very wealthy!] magician, Eliphas Levi declares that on Sunday (the day of the sun) he should carry in his right hand a golden wand, set with a ruby or chrysolite; on Monday (the day of the moon) he should wear a collar of three strands consisting of pearls, crystals, and selenites; on Tuesday (the day of Mars) he should carry a wand of magnetized steel[6] and a ring of the same metal set with an amethyst; on Wednesday (the day of Mercury) he should wear a necklace of pearls or glass beads containing mercury, and a ring set with an agate; on Thursday (the day of Jupiter) he should carry a wand of glass or resin and wear a ring set with an emerald or a sapphire; on Friday (the day of Venus) he should carry a wand of polished copper and wear a ring set with a turquoise and a crown or diadem decorated with lapis lazuli and beryl; and on Saturday (the day of Saturn) he should carry a wand ornamented with onyx stone and wear a ring set with onyx and a chain about the neck formed of lead.[7]

All of these are examples of the law of association, and depend upon similarity and contagion to produce their results. Indeed, Hall proceeds to give a long list of such associations, taken from the works of Paracelsus, Agrippa, Kircher, Lilly, "and numerous other magicians and astrologers." Here are two tables based on those paragraphs, with additions from Aleister Crowley's classic book of magical correspondences, *Liber 777*, plus some inexpensive substitutions for Crowley's suggestions.[8] (Note: Mercury and lead are very poisonous and should *not* be handled!)

Planet	Rocks
Sun	Gold, carbuncle, ruby, garnet, other fiery stones, topaz, yellow diamond, citrine
Moon	Silver, pearl, selenite, crystals, moonstone, satin spar
Mercury	Mercury, chrysolite, agate, variegated marble, fire opal, cinnabar, feather agate, tree agate
Venus	Copper, turquoise, beryl, emerald, pearl, alabaster, coral, carnelian, green malachite
Mars	Iron, amethyst, hyacinth, lodestone, diamond, ruby, desert rose, bloodstone
Jupiter	Tin, sapphire, emerald, marble, amethyst, sapphire, blue azurite, turquoise
Saturn	Lead, onyx, jasper, topaz, lapis lazuli, star sapphire, pearl, apache tear, granite, basalt

Table 8: *Astrological planet associations for metals, gems, and other stones.*

Sign	Rocks
Aries	Sardonyx, bloodstone, amethyst, diamond, ruby, red serpentine
Taurus	Carnelian, turquoise, hyacinth, sapphire, moss agate, emerald, topaz, brown obsidian
Gemini	Topaz, agate, chrysoprase, crystal, aquamarine, alexandrite, tourmaline, Iceland spar, artificial alexandrite
Cancer	Topaz, chalcedony, black onyx, moonstone, pearl, tiger eye, crystal, emerald, amber
Leo	Jasper, sardonyx, beryl, ruby, chrysolite, amber, tourmaline, diamond, tiger eye
Virgo	Emerald, carnelian, jade, chrysolite, pink jasper, hyacinth, peridot
Libra	Beryl, sardius, coral, lapis lazuli, opal, diamond, emerald, lace agate
Scorpio	Amethyst, beryl, sardonyx, aquamarine, carbuncle, lodestone, topaz, malachite, snakestone
Sagittarius	Hyacinth, topaz, chrysolite, emerald, carbuncle, turquoise, jacinth, flint
Capricorn	Chrysoprase, ruby, malachite, black onyx, white onyx, jet, moonstone, black diamond, fluorescent minerals
Aquarius	Crystal, sapphire, garnet, zircon, opal, glass, rutilated quartz
Pisces	Sapphire, jasper, chrysolite, moonstone, amethyst, pearl; fossils

Table 9: *Astrological sign associations for gems and other stones.*

The alert reader will have noticed that some stones appear in more than one planet or sign's listing. This is due to the sheer number of stones (and their sub-varieties) that exists, as well as the fact that similarity, like beauty, is in the eye of the beholder, so that different authorities made different judgment calls. Crowley's associations in particular are based on his own theories of the Christian Cabala, and his personal philosophy of Thelema.[9] Because the largest influence on the traditional beliefs about the energies of these minerals, metals, crystals, and gems, as well as their uses for healing, is their astrological associations, we must list those energies as primarily metaphorical. As a possible contrast, let's look at something a bit more modern.

New Age "Crystal Power"

One can hardly have a discussion of any New Age topic without people wanting to inject crystals of some sort into the conversation. Indeed, for most people, the concept that crystals and other unusual stones have special energies is a quintessentially New Age (or "dingbat," if you're rude) idea. However, this idea is not new; in fact, it may go all the way back to Reichenbach's experiments with charging crystals with odic force back in 1840s, and the subsequent use of crystals by mesmerists. The early Theosophists, similar to many before and after them, used crystal balls for scrying (meditative gazing) to produce clairvoyant visions. In the mid-20th century, Edgar Cayce (1887–1945), "the sleeping prophet," saw in his many trance visions that the ancient (archetypal or imaginary?) civilization of Atlantis supposedly had been powered by strange crystals.

From a mundane point of view, a crystal is created when atoms, molecules, or ions arrange themselves into particular geometrical structures of repeating internal patterns. The word "crystal" itself comes from the Greek *krystallos*, meaning "clear ice," and was originally used for what we now call quartz crystals. However, there are many other kinds of crystals, including metal crystals, salt crystals, diamonds, graphite crystals, and those comprised of various igneous rocks.

The crystals that New Agers and other modern mystics, magicians, and energy workers usually focus on are the large or especially lustrous ones. Such crystals, including quartz, amethysts, diamonds, and other precious stones, are often thought to contain enormous powers for healing and other mystical purposes. To skeptics, however, the only powers that crystals have can be chalked up to anecdotal evidence (isolated testimonials), the placebo effect (you believe that something will heal you, so it does), "group-think," wishful thinking, and other psychological factors. These factors have much more to do with what people *believe* about their crystals, than with any physical characteristics those crystals might have. Interestingly, all of these factors are actually essential for making magic work!

"But what about the piezoelectric effect?" we hear some of you asking. This very real property of some crystals is probably one of the seeds from which the idea of supposed crystal powers grew, so we should take a closer look at it. The piezoelectric effect occurs when small pieces of certain kinds of crystals produce electric currents when they are compressed, as well as when crystals actually change shape when they are subjected to an electrical current. Discovered in 1880 by Pierre and Jacques Curie, it was for several decades one of those curious scientific facts of little practical use until a few other inventions followed suit. In the first half of the 20th century, piezoelectricity was used to create sonar (underwater radar), and later for making record player[10] needles and various electronic measuring devices. Today it is the reason we have hi-tech audio equipment, ultrasound machines, lasers, and inkjet printers.

Because so many modern mystics misuse scientific terminology, the piezoelectric effect—and the way it connects crystals with energy in the mind and imagination of the mystic—seems as though it would be a prime candidate for such abuse. To the best of our knowledge, no one has managed to demonstrate a solid scientific link between piezoelectricity (or any other physical forces) and the mystical properties associated with crystals. Could it be that the only real powers that crystals have are found in the minds of those using them? Here's a paragraph by "Crystal Healer" discussing the use of crystals for healing, taken from a Website essay titled "The Science of Crystal Healing":

> The essence of the body is energy. Crystals function as transformers and amplifiers of various energies into biological energies that rebalance and re-energize our biological system on the cellular level, as well as on our emotional, mental, and spiritual levels. The premise on which this biological transfer of energy is based is that the body is a series of synchronous, oscillating, solid and liquid crystal systems to which our crystal healing techniques are able to transfer energy directly, as from one crystal to another. This transfer of energy aids the system in attaining a certain functional strength in which it can regenerate.[11]

This is a classic example of combining a bunch of scientific and technical terms in order to sound rational to anyone who doesn't know what the terms really mean. Yes, the human body is composed of energy—everything that exists is—but there are many different kinds of energy, not all of which can be modified by "transformers and amplifiers." I doubt that the reader will find many microbiologists who will agree that the body is "a series of synchronous, oscillating, solid and liquid crystal systems." This paragraph, indeed the whole essay, would be decried as nonsense by a Western-trained scientist—but that doesn't mean that the writer can't heal people by using crystals! It might simply mean that he doesn't understand how he does it, and thus makes up plausible sounding explanations. He claims to have done many experiments and clinical trials of his techniques, so it would seem that he is at least trying to be scientific. Yet, even though he hails from India, he is stuck in the Western scientific paradigm that requires him to try any explanation other than the most obvious one: it's magic.

Here's another typical New Age take on crystals, this one taken from *The Crystal Wisdom Book*, by Stephanie Harrison and Barbara Kleiner:

> Crystals have been used throughout history as tools for divination and healing. They have been revered and valued by numerous civilizations such as the Mayans and ancient Egyptians, and their use has even been recorded in the Iron Ages. They can activate, enhance and amplify all that they connect with, when used with conscious intent and knowledge. Each crystal is unique, carrying its own particular theme and frequency and each individual will respond differently to the crystal.[12]

Let's unpack this paragraph a bit. The two authors present these ideas and "facts" in order to further their theories:

+ A conflation of divination (their use as scrying objects and pendulums) and healing.

+ A reference to ancient peoples, the Mayans and Egyptians, considered by New Agers to be especially mystical, plus a vague reference to a phase of history common to most cultures (the Iron Ages).

+ A vague and undefined claim, using scientific jargon, that crystals can "activate, enhance and amplify...all that they connect with." All what? People? Places? Objects? Undefined energy fields?

The real key may be that crystals must be "used with conscious intent and knowledge." That's a reference to magic being done by the user, which he or she could also do with many other kinds of objects. So what makes crystals so special? The writers contend that "each crystal is unique, carrying its own particular theme and frequency," and "each individual will respond differently to the crystal." With such an escape clause, how can the authors be held accountable if their descriptions don't seem to match up with the reader's own personal experiences with crystals? What is a crystal's "theme," anyway? And how does the term "frequency" relate to solid objects? And finally, how useful can crystals be if the reader can't predict how they will work for him or her?

Why do people persist in believing that crystals are uniquely powerful? Here's another paragraph from the same book:

Crystals are examples of physical matter arranged in perfect symmetry; due to the regular internal and external structures. They are therefore [!] considered to be "patterns of perfection" which inspire balance and total alignment in surrounding energy fields.[13]

The first sentence is true, though somewhat exaggerated. The second doesn't say who considers them to be "patterns of perfection," or how a rock could "inspire" energy fields, or what they mean by "balance and total alignment." The paragraph that follows in the book talks about crystals' ability to inspire the user, but that's a different (albeit possibly related) matter. Later in the book, when the authors talk about "using crystals for healing," they use the analogy (one we've seen in other books on the topic) that the perfection of crystals can somehow act like a tuning fork to "give us a template of perfection to aspire to." In other words, it's mostly in the mind of the healer, and possibly of the person being healed—which is not to say that it isn't real: almost all psychic, magical, mystical, and spiritual phenomena are functions of the minds of the people involved.

More slippery metaphors are invoked when the authors try to explain how crystals actually work:

No healer or crystal heals anyone! The true healing process takes place within the person themselves. In other words, all healing is a form of self-healing. However, the crystals and the healer act as catalysts to activate this process. It is as if they act as a temporary scaffolding system to help "jump start" the patient's own healing. The crystals can also act as points of focus, shaping the universal healing energy to make it more accessible to both patient and healer.[14]

The authors don't explain how a piece of crystal could act as a catalyst for a physiological process such as healing, but we assume it is through changing the patient's aura. This sounds as if the authors are saying that crystals function mainly as magical tools (theatrical props useful in ritual) to concentrate and focus the attention of the magician on the task at hand, using the regular laws of magic. However, most New Agers are reluctant to use the vocabulary of magic—or even the word magic itself—to explain what they do. There is obviously a psychosomatic element involved as well: if patients think a doctor, nurse, or crystal healer is doing something effective, then the placebo effect kicks in and many patients heal themselves (albeit through a process that mainstream Western medicine doesn't understand).

Our suggestion that crystals work primarily through their use as magical tools is unknowingly supported by Sue and Simon Lilly in their beautiful book *Healing with Crystals and Chakra Energies*, in a section titled "Programming a Crystal":

> To direct a crystal's energy towards a specific, clearly defined goal you need to programme it. This will always be most effective when your intention matches the natural quality of the crystal. Programming a blue crystal to radiate red energy is possible, for example, but will go against the flow of energy that crystal possesses....There are two ways to programme a crystal. The first way is by exposure to a type of energy, such as a light source. A clear quartz that is exposed for a prolonged amount of time to red light, for example, will after a while begin to resonate to that red frequency. The second programming technique is to redirect the stone's energy through strong intention and affirmation. Hold the stone in your hands, or to your heart or brow, and project your intention into the centre of the crystal. Repeat this process several times

until you intuitively feel that the crystal can now hold and broadcast the thought or intention. For successful programming, it is important that the intention you project is as clear and precise as possible. Vague or muddled desires bring vague results. Once it is pro-grammed, place the crystal carefully in a space where it can be seen, to remind you of your goals.To remove the programming repeat the process with the intention that the stone reverts to its normal state. Cleanse the crystal and thank it for its help.[15]

We will leave it as an exercise for the reader to count how many laws of magic are involved in this programming process. The phraseology is designed to sound scientific (one programs computers, after all), but the authors are describing classic con-secration techniques that any magician or mystic would recog-nize. Their color association system, which is effectively used to organize their book, is based on the colors traditionally asso-ciated with different chakras (quasi-physical energy centers) in the human body (see Chapter 8 for more on these).

Please understand that we are not denying the ability of at least some crystal healers to effectively treat their patients. We are, however, asserting our belief that the use of crystals for such purposes is magical, not scientific, and is subject to all the laws of magic and other variables known to occultists for centuries. New Agers use scientific and technological metaphors because most of them are uncomfortable using the terminology of magic to describe what they do—it just sounds too primitive and superstitious. But what about that piezoelectric effect, some of you may be asking? We're afraid it's just another pseudo-scientific explanation. This effect is a very far cry from waving small or large crystals near someone and expecting to change their body's energy fields, whether these fields are occult or mundane.

Are there really special kinds of energy fields in and around crystals? We doubt it, unless the crystals have been specifically charged (in the occult sense) as magical objects by people who know how to do it. Now you can join them!

Exercise 6:
Cleansing and Charging a Crystal

Cleansing

When we cleanse something metaphysically, we are stripping off any existing vibes so that we can impose our own vibe. Cleansing is perhaps not the best description, as the goal is not so much removing dirt as it is restoring a state of neutrality. Maybe stripping paint is a closer analogy. (But saying we're teaching stripping may convey the wrong impression!)

Perhaps the most useful way to think of energy cleansing is as a process that returns the object's energy signature to a neutral state, something akin to the ground and center exercise in Chapter 4. "Neutral" does not denote a lack of energy; the quartz will still be "quartzy," and the lodestone still magnetic. What you are doing is removing all the outer layers of energy that the stone has accumulated on its journey from the Earth into your hands. The accumulated energies might be completely benign, in which case you're stripping off the old paint first before changing the wall color to what you want. If the energy accumulation is toxic or unpleasant, you're defusing it before it can interfere with your use of the object.

Similar techniques are used to cleanse many different types of objects. Depending on the circumstances, you may wish to put the object in contact with a substance that has energy-draining properties. Salt and salt water are often used this way. In many systems, salt is regarded as inimical to spirits. Just as salting the ground or food will kill anything growing on it, salting your object will get rid of any negative energy. Salting an object is considered a strong, harsh cleansing. There are physical as well as metaphysical reasons for this: some substances can actually be damaged by salt or salt water. Don't cleanse your opals in salt. Soaking the object in plain water is a gentler version of the same technique. When immersed, the object's energies will be drained off into the water. To use more metaphysical language, because water is a pure substance, the object will lose its impurities and take on the purity of the water. Just don't use the water for anything else after that, as it will no longer be pure.

Cleansing can also involve the use of kinetic energy. Kinetic energy is the energy of movement. Rapid, strong movement is supposed to scatter the energy attached to an object, dissipating it harmlessly. Kinetic techniques can involve leaving something flapping in the wind, or putting it under running water. Potent sources of kinetic energy are often used for safely disposing of items thought to contain a lot of negative energy. The ocean, especially a place with crashing waves, is a great place to toss something you want to get rid of safely. Swift rivers or waterfalls do the same. For a gentler version (and one with fewer geographical limitations), leave your object out in the rain. (Of course, you should always be mindful of local littering laws—and never throw anything potentially harmful to the environment into any body of water!)

Many folk practices take advantage of manmade kinetic generators, such as railroad tracks or busy intersections. If you place something near railroad tracks (kids, don't try this at home), the energy of the train whooshing by scatters the energy of your object. The kinetic energy of an intersection, while not as dramatic as that of a passing locomotive, has the advantage of scattering energy in more than one direction at once. The energy is dispersed, and hopefully too "confused" (note the personification) to find its way back to the object or to you.

Another possibility is to leave the object in contact with something so large that its energies are overwhelmed. This is related to our first technique, but on a bigger scale. The Earth and the ocean are so large that they can absorb anything we send them (metaphysically speaking, that is—they cope better with toxic vibes than with toxic dumps). The method is straightforward: bury the object or dump it in the water. As a rule, burying makes it easier to retrieve the object later on. Leave it in the ground for as long as seems reasonable to deal with its "crud quotient." If you toss it in the water and want it back later, you'd best work out how you're going to fish it out before you chuck it in. Again, if you try any of these techniques, it's advisable to always be mindful of local littering laws and the health of the environment.

Finally, the ultimate cleaning is purification by fire. If you're really determined to destroy something, burning it is the ultimate act—simply toss it into an open flame. However, as an old saying goes, nothing goes into the fire and emerges unchanged. Fire is an unforgiving medium. Throw a river rock into the campfire and you'll cleanse it of bad vibes, all right, but when it explodes, you might have more than bad vibes to worry about. Toss your lovely amber chunk into the fireplace, and you'll watch it change to its original matter state—resin—as it melts into a puddle and then burns away. Ashes of antique resin, while energy-neutral, are difficult to mount into jewelry. However, because we're dealing with mystical energy, symbolic acts are often just as powerful as real ones. Therefore, a safer option would be to pass your object quickly through an open flame. Candles work well for this, as long as you remember to mind your sleeves. Passing something through the swirling smoke of incense is a related technique, and one that also incorporates kinetic energy. The gentlest fire techniques would use firelight alone. Bathe the object in the glow from your fire, or better yet, combine light and heat by using natural light. Put the object (not opals, however) out in the sun, or under the light of the moon.

Now that you have brought the energy into neutral, you can shift it into something else by charging it.

Charge!

In magical energy terminology, charging means loading up something with energy and/or magic, just as you would charge a battery. The resulting energy is then available to be used later for other applications. Because we're not talking about literal electricity, however, we can't just plug something into an outlet. In fact, what we need to do is plug into a "metaphysical circuit" and transfer the energy into whatever it is you want to charge. Methods of charging could be divided roughly into two techniques: passive infusion, in which something is placed on or near an energy source in order to absorb its energy; and active transfer, in which an energy source is tapped and consciously transferred to the target. (Or, in simpler terms, one can "sap" or "zap.")

In order to passively infuse something with energy, put your cleansed object in contact with another object that has the energy signature you wish to obtain. Really, it's that simple. Passive infusion happens all the time, whether we realize it or not. The jewelry we wear every day picks up our vibe, living spaces get imprinted energetically by the people who occupy them, and people are changed by the places they frequent (which, in fact, is the basis of feng shui). Thus, the simplest method of charging a crystal, magical tool, or piece of jewelry for your personal use is keep it in close contact with yourself. Wear it, carry it in your pocket, or sleep with it under your pillow until it feels like an extension of yourself. You can also put an object in contact with something else that has the vibe you wish to impart. Snuggle your cleansed crystal up against another one. Attach a charm to the cat's collar. Leave objects in your sacred space.

Be aware that there is a rolling downhill factor to this method; larger objects will tend to overwhelm smaller objects, and active or biological energies will tend to influence inert objects. If you put a tiny crystal in contact with a great big boulder, you're most likely to wind up with the crystal charged with (or neutralized by) boulder energy—unless that little crystal has one heck of charge to begin with.

Active transfer methods requires more user participation. In this, energy is deliberately moved or transferred from a source to a target. Perhaps the easiest way to understand this technique is to imagine turning on a spigot to fill a pail with water. The water is the energy, the local water supply is the source, the bucket is the target, and you are the pipes, faucet, and faucet turner all rolled into one. You, the charger, can start, stop, and regulate the flow of water (energy) however you wish. In this analogy, it is most important to remember that you are the conduit, not the water source. In other words, don't drain your own energy to do the job; usually, energy should be transferred or channeled *through* you, not *out* of you. Think of yourself as a conduit, just as you do when you ground and center.

The most common method of active charging is to send energy out of your hands into whatever it is you want to charge. The easiest way to sense energy flowing from your hands is to practice making the energy ball (Exercise 4). In t'ai chi (which makes regular use of a ball of qi), we are told that energy follows attention. This is what allows us to focus an energy flow in a particular direction and to a particular target. *Intention* can also impart a "flavor" to the energy being deployed, allowing you to charge a stone specifically for healing or protection, for example. This sort of charging may be akin to what some call programming a crystal, although your authors have some reservations about using that terminology.

Here's a simple but effective approach to charging an object:

✦ Ground and center.

✦ Place the target to be charged in your hands. If that is not practical, place your hands above and below or on each side of the target.

✦ Let the energy you've embraced from the Earth or sky in your grounding exercise flow through you and out the palms of your hands.

✦ Through attention and concentration, focus the energy flow on the target to be charged. Make the target the center of your energy ball. Send the energy around it, through it, and into it.

✦ Release the flow, relax, and ground and center.

Plant Virtues, Signatures, and Powers

Plants are indeed virtuous, in that they hardly ever lie or cheat on their taxes, but when people in previous centuries wrote about plant virtues, they were referring to the fact that plants could be put to various mundane and magical uses, such as healing or spellcasting. Healers and magicians noticed that certain parts of certain plants seemed to have significant effects on people and animals, ones we would call "pharmacological" today. The result of many centuries' worth of these observations led to the idea that plants had inherent virtues.

Virtues were associated with the doctrine of signatures, often credited to the alchemist/physician Paracelsus (1493–1541), though it predates him by centuries. This doctrine states that plants and their parts are analogous to the body parts of humans and animals that they are best suited to treat. This variation on the magical law of similarity was invoked (if you will pardon the expression) in mostly secular terms as the natural consequences of original divine acts, either directly through the creation of plants, or indirectly through the creation of the planets and stars that influenced the plants.

In 1600, a master shoemaker in the small town of Görlitz, Germany, named Jakob Böhme (1575-1624) had a mystical vision which led him to believe that God had "signed" all of his creation with indications of what it could be used for. He wrote a book called *Signatura Rerum: The Signature of all Things*. In it, Böhme argued that the shape and color of a plant's flowers, leaves, or roots, where it grew, or even its traditional folk names, were all indicators of what it was intended to treat. For example, if a plant's flower was the same shape as a spleen, then it could be used to heal spleen problems. Likewise, if the roots resembled varicose veins, they could be boiled and made into a paste to rub into the skin over the veins to heal them. Although this might seem nonsensical in the 21st century, there are plenty of herbalists and other healers who still subscribe to this doctrine.[16]

Similar to the rocks discussed previously, plants in Western mysticism were also associated with astrological planets and signs, often based on their similarity to the planetary deities or zodiac animals. As you will soon see, different astrological signs were associated with different body parts, starting with Aries at the head and going down to Pisces at the feet. Plants thought to be useful for healing particular illnesses were then associated with the signs corresponding to the relevant parts of the body, so that the web of associations went in both directions.

Here are a few words from Barrett on the topic of plant powers:

The herb cinque-foil being gathered before sun-rise, one leaf thereof cures the ague of one day; three leaves, cures the tertian; and four, the quartan ague. Rape seeds, sown with cursings and imprecations, grows the fairer, and thrives; but if with praises, the reverse. The juice of deadly nightshade, distilled, and given in a proportionate quantity, makes the party imagine almost whatever you chuse. The herb nip, being heated in the hand, and afterwards you hold in your hand the hand of any other party, they shall never quit you, so long as you retain that herb. The herbs arsemart, comfrey, flaxweed, dragon-wort, adder's-tongue, being steeped in cold water, and if for some time being applied on a wound, or ulcer, they grow warm, and are buried in a muddy place, cureth the wound, or sore, to which they were applied.[17]

Hall's *Secret Teachings of All Ages* also explains that plants can have many powers, both mystical and mundane:

> The great variety of flora made it possible to find some plant or flower which would be a suitable figure for nearly any abstract quality or condition. A plant might be chosen because of some myth connected with its origin, as the stories of Daphne and Narcissus; because of the peculiar environment in which it thrived, as the orchid and the fungus; because of its significant shape, as the passion flower and the Easter lily; because of its brilliance or fragrance, as the verbena and the sweet lavender; because it preserved its form indefinitely, as the everlasting flower; because of unusual characteristics as the sunflower and heliotrope, which have long been sacred because of their affinity for the sun. The plant might also be considered worthy of veneration because from its crushed leaves, petals, stalks, or roots could be extracted healing unctions, essences, or drugs affecting the nature and intelligence of human beings—such as the poppy and the ancient herbs of prophecy. The plant might also be regarded as efficacious in the cure of many diseases because its fruit, leaves, petals, or roots bore a resemblance in shape or color to parts or organs of the human body. For example, the distilled juices of certain species of ferns, also the hairy moss growing upon oaks, and the thistledown were said to have the power of growing hair; the dentaria, which resembles a tooth in shape, was said to cure the toothache; and the palma Christi plant, because of its shape, cured all afflictions of the hands.[18]

So what we have from both authors are examples of plants working magically, through similarity and contagion, as well as medicinally, through their pharmacological effects. In the case of the former, the energies involved would seem to reside mostly in the mind of the healer or magician. In the latter case, the energies are biochemical ones, though these may cause changes in the mystical or mundane energies in the bodies of those being treated.

Table 10 on page 192 and Table 11 on page 193 are two more tables based on Barrett and Hall, with additions from Aleister Crowley's classic book of magical correspondences, *Liber 777*. (Note: Do not use these or any other herbal remedies without proper medical supervision.)

There is little evidence to indicate that Westerners thought of non-hallucinogenic plants as having energies beyond their related astrological ones, or the vaguely defined life force inhabiting healthy plants. Chinese traditions, although just as complex in their understanding of the uses of herbs as those in the West, were based more on the Chinese Element system, as well as on theories regarding the amount of qi (and its yin or yang orientation) in each species. All plants have biochemical energies inside them, and something on the outside resembling the auras or energy fields seen in humans and other animals. There are some very famous Kirlian photographs[19] of leaves with sections cut away, that seem to depict an energy field where the missing parts had originally been. (A critique of this technique contends that the energy fields could just as easily have been the accidental result of the way the leaves were prepared and photographed.)

Planet	Plants	Animals
Sun	Pine, acacia, bay, laurel, vine, heliotrope, calendula, St. John's Wort, sunflower, dandelion	Hawk, sparrowhawk, rooster, phoenix, lion, tiger
Moon	Cleavers, catnip, caraway, banyan, mandrake, damiana, yohimbe, almond, mugwort, hazel, moonworth, ranunculus	Cat, deer, pig, elephant, dog, wolf
Mercury	Moly, *anhalonium lewinii*, vervain, marjolane, palm	Jackal, dog, swallow, ibis, ape, twin serpents
Venus	Rose, myrtle, clover	Fish, dove, lynx, sparrow, swan
Mars	Oak, *nux vomica*, nettle, absinth, rue	Rooster, hippo, basilisk, horse, bear, wolf
Jupiter	Olive, shamrock, hyssop, fig, poplar	Eagle, bull, unicorn
Saturn	Cypress, opium poppy, oak, ivy, almond tree (in flower), mandrake	Bull, sphinx

Table 10: *Astrological planet associations for plants and animals.*

The only other sorts of "powers" associated with plants are the spirits that may be connected to them, including devas, deities, and totems. Plant devas are anthropomorphic (human-like) spirits that represent the mystical properties of different plant species, particularly hallucinogens. Examples would include San Mescalito, the spirit of peyote, and Bella Donna ("fair lady"), the spirit associated with the belladonna plant. Plant totems are plant-related spirits who may be seen as mystically

Sign	Plants	Animals
Aries	Tiger lily, geranium	Sheep, owl
Taurus	Mallow	Cow
Gemini	Hybrids, orchids	Magpie, all hybrids, monkey, butterfly, parrot
Cancer	Lotus	Crab, turtle, sphinx, lobster
Leo	Sunflower	Lion, tiger, leopard
Virgo	Snowdrop, lily, narcissus	All pets, especially dogs and cats
Libra	Aloe	Elephant, all reptiles
Scorpio	Cactus	Scorpion, serpent, eagle, crayfish, wolf, lobster, beetle, all other insects
Sagittarius	Rush	Centaur, horse, hippogriff, dog
Capricorn	Hemp, orchis root, thistle	Goat, ass
Aquarius	Olive, coconut	Eagle, peacock
Pisces	Opium	Fish, seal, dolphin, crayfish, beetle, all microbes

Table 11: *Astrological sign associations for plants and animals.*

ancestral to particular tribes, while plant deities are divine personifications of particular species, such as Corn Woman or Bean Woman among the Native Americans, or Jack-in-the-Green and John Barleycorn among Neo-Pagans. Of course, plants can be used in magical or religious rituals, both as incense sources and as symbols of particular deities or other spirits who might happen to prefer particular plants, so we could very loosely describe such uses as involving the plants' energies.

Animal Powers

Similar to plants and rocks, animals have been credited with natural and supernatural powers by people all over the world. Certainly they remain powerful sources of symbolism. Phrases such as "a wolf at the door," "sly as a fox," "acting like sheep," "brave as a lion," and so on reflect accumulated common wisdom (much of it erroneous) about the various species of animals with whom we share our planet.

Here's what Barrett has to say about animals in Chapter 7 of *The Magus*:

It is expedient for us to know that there are some things which retain virtue only while they are living, others even after death. So in the cholic, if a live duck be applied to the belly, it takes away the pain, and the duck dies. If you take the heart out of any animal, and, while it is warm, bind it to one that has a quartan fever, it drives it away. So if any one shall swallow the heart of a lapwing, swallow, weasel, or a mole, while it is yet living and warm with natural heat, it improves his intellect, and helps him to remember, understand, and foretel things to come. Hence this general rule, that whatever things are taken for magical uses from animals, whether they are stones, members, hair, excrements, nails, or any thing else, they must be taken from those animals while they are yet alive, and, if it is possible, that they may live afterwards. If you take the tongue of a frog, you put the frog into water again; and Democritus writes, that if any one shall take out the tongue of a water-frog, no other part of the animal sticking to it, and lay it upon the place where the heart beats of a woman, she is compelled, against her will, to answer whatsoever you shall ask of her. Also, take the eyes of a frog, which must be extracted before sun-rise, and bound to the sick party, and the frog to be let go again blind into the water, the party shall be cured of a tertian ague; also, the same will, being bound with the flesh of a nightingale in the skin of a hart, keep a person always wakeful without sleeping. Also, the roe of the fork fish being bound to the navel, is said to cause women an easy child-birth, if it be taken from it alive, and the fish put into the sea again. So the right eye of a serpent being applied to the soreness of the eyes, cures the same, if the serpent be let go alive. So, likewise, the tooth of a mole, being taken out alive, and afterwards let go, cures the tooth-ache; and dogs will never bark at those who have the tail of a weasel that has escaped. Democritus says, that if the tongue of the chameleon be taken alive, it conduces to good success in trials, and like-wise to women in labour; but it must be hung up on some part of the outside of the house, otherwise, if brought into the house, it might be most dangerous. There are very many properties that remain after death; and these are things in which the idea of the matter is less swal-lowed up, according. to Plato, in them: even after death, that which is immortal in them will work some wonder-ful things: as in the skins we have mentioned of several wild beasts, which will corrode and eat one another af-ter death; also, a drum made of the rocket-fish drives away all creeping things at what distance soever the sound of it is heard; and the strings of an instrument made of the guts of a wolf, and being strained upon a harp or lute, with strings made of sheep-guts, will make no harmony.[20]

(Author's note: It should go without saying that you shouldn't try any of Barrett's suggestions at home!)

Somehow, we don't think this is exactly what New Agers and Neo-Pagans have in mind when they talk about mystical animal powers! Such messy (and cruel) use of animal parts is very unappealing to the modern mind, though it is very clear that these spells are using the principles of contagion and similarity. Modern magicians, mystics, and energy workers see animals as spiritual partners and teachers representing particular characteristics that they wish to develop or suppress within themselves.

As Philip and Stephanie Carr-Gomm say in *The Druid Animal Oracle Deck*:

> "Somehow animals act as ideal symbols or images of our deepest fears and urges, or of those parts of our psyche which have been denied or repressed or simply neglected. By welcoming and loving the animals which enter our awareness through the Oracle, in dreams and meditations and reverie, we enrich our inner world and discover a way of personal growth that is completely in tune with the natural world.[21]

There are people who believe themselves to be part animal, or animal souls that have been incarnated in human bodies, much as some transgendered people believe themselves to be women in men's bodies or vice versa. These "transspecies" people call themselves "therians." Another group believes themselves to be mythical animals, or even aliens or faeries in human form, and refer to themselves as "otherkin." Some therians develop very close and loving relationships with their animal "relatives," and become active in animal protection movements. Perhaps not surprisingly, some experience difficulty in relating to other human beings. Some therians belong to the "furry" subculture of people who enjoy "stories, film, plays and artwork about animals with human characteristics,"[22] and dress up and role-play as other species of animals. Members of the New Age, Neo-Shamanic movement devote a lot of effort to connecting with the spiritual essence of other animals; they often point to cave paintings of men dressed as (or mating with) animals as evidence that Paleolithic peoples considered themselves far closer to their animal counterparts than most humans do today. Whether people in any of these groups should be considered deeply mystical, fascinating thinkers, animal-human relationship pioneers, psychologically dysfunctional, or something else entirely, is up to the reader to decide.

Certainly if you spend enough time observing and interacting closely with other animals, you can gradually make yourself more like them, and possibly learn such virtues as patience, tenacity, cooperation, loyalty, and so on. We have no doubt that many animals are more virtuous than humans, but Phaedra has noticed that humans tend to project their own psychological issues and cultural expectations onto animals—hence the common scholarly nonsense about birds being "monogamous," or wolves committing "adultery," that has appeared in academic journals for generations. (At least until DNA analysis of offspring showed that other animals "mess around" at least as often as humans do!)

Part
III

Energies From
People and Spirits

Chapter 7

Paranormal and Psychic Powers

What Do These Terms Mean?

As we mentioned in Chapter 1, the term "psychic" was attached to the various phenomena—items floating in the air, weird sounds, clairvoyant visions—produced by mediums in the 19th century, and by the people then known as psychical researchers (now known as parapsychologists). Today, parapsychologists study the whole range of paranormal (literally, "beyond the normal") activities: ESP, hypercognition, and psychokinesis, as well as various phenomena associated with ghosts, reincarnation, and other "supernatural" topics. If these researchers knew about them, they might also study what Isaac calls the "anti-psi" powers.

Many people use such terms as psychic talents, psi skills, psionic abilities, and so on with varying degrees of precision and interchangeability. To us, these terms all refer to exactly the same concept—particular (and sometimes peculiar) abilities to perceive and/or manipulate subtle energies and information by conscious or subconscious intent, producing results that are inexplicable by this week's scientific wisdom.

"Psionic" was a term invented by science-fiction author and editor John Campbell back in the mid-20th century as a way to avoid using the terms "psychic" or "magical," so that authors who didn't believe in such things could still write about them with scientific-sounding vocabulary. Many New Age writers with scientific backgrounds (or pretensions) use the term psionic for the same reasons sci-fi authors do—they don't want to admit that what they are doing is psychic or magical.

The term "psi" is just an abbreviation for "psychic," but it's also the name of the Greek letter (Ø) with which the word "psyche" begins. By itself, psi has a broader meaning connected to all those energies and experiences traditionally called "psychic" by parapsychologists and other researchers. There are paraphysicists (parapsychologists who are also physicists) who believe that psi is a category of energy, just as electromagnetism and gravity are, and thus has a connection to the other quantum forces. Perhaps its unit of measurement could then be called "psions," similar to the photons of light.

Psi or psychic energy may comprise a part or all of what we've been generically calling mystical energy in this book, and which Isaac has called mana in others. We agree with the paraphysicists that psi energy is a natural force distributed throughout the universe(s), just as light, gravity, and the strong and weak nuclear forces are. According to Isaac's observations, psi can be converted into and from other natural forces, and can be used by both natural and supernatural beings (if indeed the word "supernatural" has any real meaning at all). It may or may not have anything to do with dark energy or dark matter, though we've been having fun with these concepts in this book.

Ironically, psychic energy is what Hans Berger (the man who invented what we now call the EEG machine) had in mind when he began his inquiries into neurology. He was looking specifically for an energy that would explain the life-changing telepathic or hypercognitive communication he had experienced with his sister.

Varieties of Psychic Talents

Although there are many different psi talents known to us by research and/or experience, they can all be grouped into four major categories with some overlap. These are: Extra-sensory perception, or ESP, which refers to a variety of psi talents involving the reception of external data through other than the commonly recognized sensory means (though the reception often seems to be sensory); hypercognition, which refers to the psi talent or talents responsible for what most people call intuition or hunches; psychokinesis, or PK, which refers to a variety of psi talents that involve the inexplicable movement of matter and energy via the conscious or subconscious will of a person; and anti-psi, which refers to psi talents that modify or cancel out other psi talents. Let's look at a few of these very briefly.

Extra-Sensory Perception

Telepathy is the communication of information from one mind to another without the use of the normal sensory channels. Telepathic sending and receiving probably constitute distinct talents, although they are usually found together in one person. Empathy is the telepathic reception of emotional data, and mesmerism (named after Franz Mesmer) is a form of telepathic communication, in which the data communicated consists of hypnotic suggestions.

Clair-sensing is the reception of sensory data under circumstances that would make normal sensing impossible. This comes in several forms: Clairvoyance (now called remote viewing by some parapsychologists) is the most common form, and involves visions in which one psychically "sees" events or objects. Clairaudience, the next most common form, involves hearing voices or other sounds in a paranormal manner. And in clairtangency, clairolfaction, and clairgustance, respectively, refer to the paranormal reception of information about an object (or an object's owner) simply by touching, smelling, or tasting it.

Psychometry,[1] sometimes also called clairsentience, clairempathy, or object reading, is a talent that should not be confused with the other "clair" senses, although it frequently works with them. It is the ability to receive data from objects or surroundings regarding events or persons connected to those objects or surroundings. It may very well be that psychometry is not an independent talent at all, but merely the ability to use objects or surroundings as links for telepathic reception and/or retrocognition. The magical law of contagion would seem to have a direct application to this particular psi talent.

Out-of-body experiences (or OOBEs) involve the sensation of one's consciousness being outside of one's physical body, usually as a moveable entity. There are two main kinds of OOBEs: In astral projection, one travels in an astral body (vehicle of consciousness) that is similar to one's physical body. The astral body is usually translucent or invisible, lightweight, and capable of flight, and can pass through ordinary matter, including lead, gold, and silver. It is often immune to temperature or a vacuum, and can supposedly move faster than light. Mental projection is very similar to astral projection, except that no body seems to be carted around.

No one knows whether the astral body, and the so-called astral planes this body may travel in from time to time, is a multisensory hallucination, or if it represents a different but related form and level of our normal physical reality. Most mystics believe the latter. As the alert reader may recall from a previous chapter, there are said to be many layers in the astral plane, all arranged in increasing vibratory frequency, and each one more difficult to get to than the one beneath (though all of them interpenetrate each other). Some people say that the way to rise through the planes is actually through shifting one's attention to increasingly subtle levels of reality that are all present in the same space and time.

Hypercognition

This psi talent seems to consist of very rapid thinking, usually at a subconscious level, using data received through ESP. This information is then presented to the conscious mind as a sudden awareness of knowledge without an accompanying sensory experience. When information is received in this manner regarding events or states of existence in the past, present, or future, the terms used are retrocognition, hypercognition, and precognition, respectively. All of these are easily confused with the "clair" senses, which are also capable of looking into the past, present or future, but involve visions, voices, and so on.

Psychokinesis

PK refers to the movement, through psychic means, of objects and people. There are some researchers who believe that our very ability to move our bodies at will (the mind-body link) is actually related to some form of PK. When PK proper is combined with mass control and/or gravity control, the result is often called levitation, which is usually defined as "floating or flying PK."

Recurrent spontaneous psychokinesis (or RSPK) is the modern term for what used to be called poltergeists (literally, "noisy spirits") back when this was thought to be a supernatural phenomena. Now we know that RSPK is a sort of psychic temper tantrum indulged in by people (usually adolescents) who are becoming neurotic due to repressed emotional and/or sexual energy. This energy is converted to various forms of PK, which can cause bizarre, but usually trivial, damage to the environment.

Other Categories of PK

The term apportation is used for the seemingly instantaneous movement of an object from one location in space-time to another, apparently without having to travel through the normal space-time continuum. When this occurs with a person, the process is called teleportation. Cellular psychokinesis (CPK) is a general term for what is probably the use of several different kinds of PK to affect the structure and behavior of living organisms, working primarily on the cellular level. Atomic psychokinesis is a categorical term for several psi talents that involve matter and energy at the molecular, atomic, or subatomic levels. Mass control refers to the ability to increase or decrease the mass of an object. In a gravity well (on a planet, for example), this becomes weight control, which can be difficult to distinguish from gravity control (the ability to alter the gravitational fields in a particular location—say, in a room or around an object or person). Any of these talents can be used with PK proper to produce levitation. Magnetic control is the psychic control of magnetic, diamagnetic, and paramagnetic lines of force. Electric control is the use of psi to control electricity and other electron phenomena. Light control, as its name implies, is the psi talent concerned with the control of light (that is, of photons). And temperature control is the ability to alter the speed of atoms and molecules so as to change the temperature of an object.

The Anti-psi Talents

Anti-psi is a categorical term for psi talents that operate primarily by affecting other psi talents. Several of these antipsi talents seem to involve the generation of certain psi fields to alter the content, direction, or power levels of other psychic energy fields. Catapsi is the generation of a psychic field of "static" in order to disrupt the data of other psychic energy fields. Similarly, splodging"is a kind of psychic yelling meant to drown out competing data. Apopsi is the generation of a field into which other psi fields cannot enter, possibly accomplished by changing these other fields into other forms of energy or apporting them elsewhere. Deflection alters the directions (force vectors) of incoming psychic energies and sends them elsewhere; if they are reversed 180 degrees, the talent can be called returning or reddopsi. Negapsi, or inverting, is the generation of a psi field in which all or most of the information content (data) of an incoming psychic field is reversed, thus turning creative energies or blessings into destructive energies or curses, for example. Filtering is the ability to use apopsi or deflection selectively, thus allowing only certain portions of an incoming psi field to come through. Almost everyone can do self-tuning to alter the information content of their own psi fields; if this is done to someone else's field, it is called re-tuning. Finally, the talent for boosting energy fields is called amplification, and dampening for lowering them (also called amping or damping).

Are These Abilities Real?

Our answer, based on two lifetimes of research and practice, is an unequivocal yes! At least some of the time, psychic talents appear to be very real indeed. Although the names of many of these talents were coined by Isaac in *Real Magic* back in 1971, history and laboratory experiments bear them out as real, over and over again. Cynics may complain all they like that certain psychics, such as Uri Geller, are fakes or cheats, but Isaac has watched silverware and keys writhing and bending without anyone touching them, after he and his first wife had come home from one of Geller's performances. We've both done our own informal psychic experiments over the years, such as sending Tarot cards telepathically, or trying to bless or heal houseplants, with results that far exceeded mere coincidence. Of course, we didn't have million-dollar research budgets like the folks working for the CIA or the KGB, nor did we publish our results in peer-reviewed scientific journals, as members of the American Parapsychological Association have done.

Fortunately, professional parapsychologists have done quite a bit of such high-end research and published such papers, showing over and over again that something is going on that can't be explained away by the envious or the cynical. In his book *Entangled Minds*, Dean Radin makes this very clear through his discussion of the meta-analyses (studies of previous studies) of thousands of parapsychological experiments performed by scores of researchers, over the last 50 years. A meta-analysis combines the results of several studies that address a set of related hypotheses. In other words, a statistician looks at the odds of groups of experiments by different researchers that produce significant statistical probabilities way above chance. This method has been used in psychology, sociology, and other social sciences in order to eliminate experimenter bias from multiple studies on specific topics.

Say that groups of researchers in different countries all try similar psychic experiments with hundreds of experimental subjects over a period of decades, and calculate the odds against mere chance as being anywhere from 50,000-to-one to 500,000-to-one. A meta-analysis of their work may result in odds of several billion-to-one (or higher) that coincidence, fraud, or incompetence are at play in all or most of them. As Isaac likes to put it, there are three magical laws of statistics: once is dumb luck, twice is coincidence, and three times is Somebody trying to tell you Something. When honest and unbiased psychic researchers get small but steady results year after year, and under circumstances antithetical to most psychic phenomena, those small results add up to big numbers. Perhaps the only people still refusing to allow the reality of psychic phenomena are those with emotional, intellectual, and/or financial investments in their beliefs—a topic we will save for another book. In the meantime, we highly recommend the book *Entangled Minds* for a complete overview of meta-analyses applied to parapsychological research.

As for defining what's real, that's a job for philosophers. We mystical types will happily stick with the magical law of pragmatism: If something works (on whatever level of reality that concerns you), then it's true on that level.

Active and Passive Psychic Talents

Psi as a type of energy is a vague term that may not correctly apply to every psychic talent. As the name implies, ESP is mostly a matter of perception—that is, the reception and classification of information—and it may not necessarily involve unusual energy of any sort. Similarly, hypercognition is another mental process that may or may not involve a unique kind of energy. With PK, on the other hand, mental intention alone produces a change in the physical environment (such as affecting dice throws, random number generators, or electromagnetic fields), so this must involve some type of energy that can interact with and affect energies that constitute, or are a manifestation of, physical reality. Antipsi powers may or may not involve one or more kinds of energy that we would categorize as psi.

Perhaps the answer to all of this lies in the distinction between active and passive psychic talents, in which the former involve actively changing reality, and the latter passively receiving information. If psi is a type of energy at least some of the time, then what is it? The so-called dark energy? And are the passive psychic talents more a matter of quantum relationships than energy transfer? Only future research will tell.

Chapter 8

Esoteric Anatomy and Physiology

Silly Questions, Interesting Answers

How many bodies do you have? How many souls or spirits? Are the observable parts of our bodies—the ones that surgeons can remove or repair—the only important parts? These may seem like silly questions, but esoteric traditions all around the world have come up with some fascinating answers to them.

In ancient Egypt it was believed that people had five different non-physical aspects to their being: the *ka*, or intellectual/creative power; the *ba*, or personality/ego; the *akh*, or union of the first two after death; the *ren*, or true name; and the *shwt*, or shadow (meaning the actual physical shadow cast by the sun or moon). Knowing someone's true name gave you magical power over them, hence the magical law of names. Likewise, taking dirt from the ground on which someone's shadow was cast gave you a direct magical link to them, via the law of contagion.

According to Max Freedom Long, the chronicler and creator of the Huna system of magic,[1] the ancient Hawaiian magician-priests called *kahunas* ("holders of the secret") believed that everyone had three selves in addition to their physical body. The low self—what people might refer to today as the inner child or subconscious mind—resided in the belly. The middle self was the conscious, adult mind, and resided in the head. The high self was a dual-gendered super-consciousness that resided in the air over one's head. The three selves were said to incarnate together to accomplish specific tasks set for them between lives by the Gods. They might stick together through several incarnations, or split apart to join new triads. In time, low selves would eventually get promoted to middle selves, and middle selves to high selves, and high selves to deities.

The three selves were said to be composed of a psychic substance called *aka*, which Long likened to sticky ectoplasm (the same substance through which ghosts manifest themeselves, according to Spiritualism). Along cords made of aka, magical or spiritual power called *mana* would flow like water or electricity, carrying the intent of one or more of the three selves. Interestingly, Long claimed that the middle self could not talk directly to the high self, but needed to communicate to it via the low self. This representation is a pretty good image for the metaphysical principle that the subconscious mind seems to control the gates to superconsciousness and its psychic powers.

Isaac likes to call Long "the Gerald Gardner of Hawaiian Paganism" because he suspects that Long simply made up stuff out of thin air; moreover, Long credited the ancient Hawaiians with concepts that were as much European as they were Polynesian. Much of his writing was supposedly based on his studies of the Hawaiian language (using a dictionary written by

Christian missionaries). The fact is that it involved a great deal of pseudo-linguistic nonsense. However, as with the modern creation of Wicca, Long ended up creating what he was describing.[2] For example, in the early 1970s, Isaac met a native Hawaiian who claimed to be a kahuna. The man said that his family had been kahunas in past generations, but had long since forgotten all about it. When the man discovered Long's books, he then "recovered the lost secrets." Today there are scores—if not hundreds—of people calling themselves kahunas, all working from Long's imaginative visions.

Another modern version of an ancient energy-working system was founded in Japan in the 19th century by a Dr. Mikao Usui, who called his methods for channeling ki for healing purposes *usui skiki ryoho*, now usually just called *reiki*. This system stresses the idea that the healer is not using his or her own ki except to gather, focus (through the use of specific symbols), and direct a universal life force energy or God force, which is probably the same thing as ki or qi. Reiki is similar to Wicca in that there are three levels of training to become a reiki master, no central authorities, lots of enthusiastic experimenters, feuds between practitioners, and lots of conflicting stories regarding history and initiatory lineage.

Unlike most modern body-working systems, reiki healings supposedly can be done at a distance, often of many miles, and without the recipient having to do anything special to receive the energy. The energies go where they are needed and do whatever they are supposed to do, without conscious attention by either the healer or the recipient. Some reiki masters claim that they heal but don't cure. By this they mean that they strengthen the recipient's own healing forces and/or immune system, and restore balance to the body, but they can't destroy germs or fix the emotional problems that may be causing an illness. Reiki has exploded in popularity over the past 15 years or so, and sometimes it seems as though half the New Agers on the planet claim to be reiki masters.

Now let's take a look at some other esoteric approaches to healing, and theories of how the physical and the mystical overlap in the human body.

Astrological Associations

Sign	Body Parts/Systems/Complaints
Aries	Head, brain, fevers
Taurus	Throat, lower jaw, vocal chords, neck and upper spine, thyroid,
Gemini	Shoulders, chest, upper back and spine, arms, hands, lungs, nervous system
Cancer	Breasts, stomach, liver, diaphragm, uterus, mucous membranes,
Leo	Middle back and spine, heart, fatigue
Virgo	Belly, intestines, spleen, pancreas
Libra	Kidneys, skin, lower back and spine
Scorpio	Colon, genitals, bladder, rectum
Sagittarius	Hips, tailbone, thighs, liver
Capricorn	Knees, joints, hair, skin, nails, teeth
Aquarius	Lower legs, ankles, blood circulation, rare illnesses
Pisces	Feet, toes, lymph nodes, mysterious illnesses

Table 12: *Astrological sign associations for body parts, systems, and complaints.*

Just as astrologers have traditionally associated different signs, planets, and houses with various kinds of stones, plants, and animals, they have also assigned them to different parts and systems of the human body, as well as the illnesses those parts are subject to. Table 12 shows some of the traditional body parts, systems, and complaints associated with the astrological signs.[3]

Planet	Medical Problems
Sun	Inflammations, fevers, infections, general weakness and fatigue
Moon	Psychological problems, allergies, water retention, menstrual complaints
Mercury	Problems with nerves, breathing, speech, intellect
Venus	Growths, diabetes, poor circulation in veins, venereal diseases
Mars	Those of the sun, plus blood diseases, wounds, burns, muscle problems, sudden ailments
Jupiter	Obesity, gigantism or dwarfism, liver problems, poor circulation in arteries
Saturn	Cancers, obstructions, atrophies, skin diseases, hardening or thickening of organs, chronic ailments
Uranus	Fits, convulsions, sudden illnesses, injuries caused by explosions or shocks, epilepsy, heart palpitations, stress
Neptune	Alcoholism, addictions, hidden illnesses, immune disorders, comas
Pluto	Malignant tumors, amputations, major infections, malformations, birth defects

Table 13: *Astrological planetary associations for medical problems.*

Medical astrologers (yes, this really is a recognized specialty) usually look for diseases or other problems by looking at what planets are currently in hard aspects (squares, oppositions, and so on) to each other, based on the signs those planets rule (see Chapter 4). Otherwise they look for planets being afflicted (in signs where they don't usually belong), and associate them with particular problems, as shown in Table 13 on page 215.

Those with a background in astrology will understand why these associations are structured as they are. As the planet associated with war, Mars would most logically be associated with wounds, burns, and other injuries likely to be encountered on a battlefield. Venus, the planet of love, would naturally rule diseases contracted by those who are unlucky in their choice of one or more lovers.

Western astrology does not postulate any special energy fields in or around the body; at most it implies that the planetary and sign energies and relationships are somehow connected to specific organs and systems in a way that makes medical astrology, when practiced by a trained specialist, a useful source of information about possible physiological and psychological problems. Does this mean that you should go to an astrologer instead of your regular healer? Heck, no! But if your regular healer can't figure out what's wrong with you, consulting a medical astrologer might give you some useful hints as to where the problem may lie. Just don't tell your doctor *why* you want that liver function or insulin test!

Chinese Theories

Not surprisingly, Traditional Chinese Medicine (TCM) is rooted in the esoteric (to us Westerners, anyway) concept of qi, which we already explored a bit in Chapter 5, as well as accumulated herbal and medicinal knowledge—though even that knowledge is often thought of in terms of how it affects bodily qi. The Chinese believe that living things are alive because of the qi flowing through them, and that illnesses occur when the qi becomes unbalanced or stagnant instead of flowing smoothly. The practice of acupuncture is designed to stimulate the correct amount and direction of qi throughout the body via *jing luo* (channels or meridians that seem invisible to Western scientists). As with other energy workers, acupuncturists don't think of what they do as curing as much as restoring the body's natural flow of qi, which enables the patient to heal him- or herself.

There are 14 interconnected meridians on each side of the body. They surface on the skin at 360 or so points, which acupuncturists stimulate by poking with very fine needles, and acupressure practitioners stimulate with deep tissue massage. These points are usually found in the hollows and crevices of muscles and joints, and are thought of as two-way openings through which qi can flow in or out of the body.

According to Elizabeth Moran and Val Biktashev in their book, *The Complete Idiot's Guide to Feng Shui*:

> Electrical properties of the shin along channels and points are different than nonchannel or point locations.... Scientists have observed consistent characteristics of an independent electrical conduit in the body. This conduit works with the nervous system but does not follow all of its rules. This suggests a separate system of circulating energy that is different yet interactive with the nervous

and cardiovascular systems that have been well observed and studied in conventional medicine.[4]

Some acupuncturists stimulate the points by wiggling or twirling the needles, or by running a very low electrical current through them. Apparently the meridians react to magnetic as well as electrical stimulation, which would fit with the experiments of Anton Mesmer and Baron von Reichenbach.

In the lower belly lies the *dan tien* (called the *hara* in Japan), which is the center of one's physical and spiritual balance. All movements in t'ai chi are directed from this point, with the rest of the body seen as an extension of it. T'ai chi is sometimes seen as a long-term way to get some or all of the benefits of acupuncture or acupressure, as it guides the body through almost all of its possible movements. This not only gives an internal massage to all of the organs, but also stimulates the qi to flow properly, thus dissolving away any blocks or pools of stagnant qi. T'ai chi training is usually combined with qi gong exercises, as proper breathing is an important part of all the Eastern martial arts. Certainly breathing can alter the levels of oxygen in your bloodstream, with subsequent effects on the rest of your body.

Hindu Theories

The chakra system comes from the ancient Vedic peoples of India. The *yogis*, masters of various spiritual disciplines (literally, "yokes"), discovered that different areas of the body seemed to have non-physical organs. They called these organs chakras ("wheels") because they were perceived as spinning whorls of energy and/or the wheels on a spiritual chariot, or means of progress. The chakra system was discovered by modern Westerners when

Sir John Woodroffe (1865–1936), writing as Arthur Avalon, translated two Sanskrit Tantric texts (the *Sat-Cakra-Nirupana* and the *Padaka-Pancaka*) as part of his book, *The Serpent Power*. The system of seven chakras described in these texts, which were part of the *Shakti* or Goddess movement in ancient India, was adopted by Theosophists, members of the New Thought movement, and many current New Agers.

In this system there are said to be seven main chakras along the spine, counting up from one near the tailbone to one at the top of the head, as shown in Table 14 on page 220.

In addition to these seven centers, there are said to be two spiral pathways, called *ida* and *pingali*, running vertically around the spine (similar to the sides of the DNA molecule). In the root chakra, a particular kind of energy called the *kundalini* can be found. This is visualized as a sleeping serpent, which the yogi attempts to rouse into action so that it will climb up the ida and pingali to the crown chakra and thus produce transcendental bliss and divine awareness. Some teachers in India and elsewhere say that there are eight or nine major chakras, plus minor ones in the hands and feet.

Closely connected to the concepts we are discussing here is the idea of *prana*, which is Sanskrit for "breath." This is seen as a mystical energy that is part of nature and supports all life, much like qi. Prana flows throughout the body via channels called *nadi*, much like the Chinese meridians. Two of these nadis, the ida and pingali, are wrapped around the *sushumna*—the central channel along which the chakras are strung like beads.

Esoteric Vedic (and later, Hindu and Tantric) physiology postulates that we have multiple bodies, which are layers or

Chakra Number	Sanskrit Name	English Name	Location	Associations	Physiological Notes	Color
7	Sahasrara	Crown	Top of head	Thought, divine connection, knowledge, transcendence, bliss, pure awareness	Pituitary gland, thalamus, hypothalamus	Violet or white
6	Ajna	Third eye	Brow	Light, vision, psychic powers, intuition, time	Pineal gland, melatonin	Indigo
5	Vishuddha	Throat	Throat	Sound, communication, creativity, language	Thyroid gland, growth	Blue
4	Anahata	Heart	Heart	Air, social links, love, balance, union of opposites, peace	Thymus, immune system	Green
3	Manipura	Belly	Solar plexus	Fire, power, ego, will, discipline	Pancreas, outer part of adrenal glands, digestion	Yellow
2	Swadhisthana	Sacral	Groin	Water, emotions, sexuality, desire, changeability	Genitals, sex hormones	Orange
1	Mulashara	Root or base	Tailbone	Earth, survival, grounding, health, wealth, security	Perineum, inner area of adrenal glands	Red

Table 14: *The Chakra System*

sheaths over our spiritual essence—the *atman*, or divine self. These bodies are: the *annamaya kosa* (physical body); the *pranamaya kosa* (the "vital air sheath"); the *manomaya kosa* (the "mental sheath"); the *vigyanamaya kosa* (the "intellectual sheath"); and the *karanamaya kosa* (the "causal sheath"). The second of these, the pranamaya kosa, is composed of five main varieties of prana: prana in the general sense, plus *apana*, *vyana*, *udana*, and *samana*. These are considered the vital currents generated by the human body that govern different physiological functions, including heartbeat, circulation, breathing, elimination of wastes, the voluntary muscles, hearing, digestion, metabolism, and body heat. The last kind of prana, samana, is the one responsible for the *aura* (the "body of light"). The pranamaya kosa sheath constitutes what Theosophists and New Agers refer to as the etheric body—the blueprint and sustainer of the body that functions on the etheric plane at a vibration that is higher than anything on the physical plane. In their writings, Madame Blavatsky, Alice Bailey, Colonel Woolcott, and other early leaders of the Theosophical Society appropriated many of these ideas, and concluded that people had multiple bodies, each operating at a different vibration on a different plane of existence. All of these bodies were thought to be connected to the physical body, and visible (to those who had eyes to see) as an aura of light surrounding the physical body.

All of these ideas heavily influenced Western occult traditions and later the New Age movement. It's important to remember, however, that modern New Age writers, Anodea Judith[5] foremost among them, have expanded the meaning of the original chakra system, turning it into an entire alternate healing modality. While traditional Hindu and Tantric teachers seemed to think that the chakras were states of consciousness as much as anything else, modern researchers have noted how closely they seem to be situated to major nerve and gland centers. Clearly, focusing one's awareness on these locations in does seem to stimulate their corresponding body parts and systems. But does this imply that these energies are specifically mystical?

It can be argued that the mind-body connection is itself dependent on some sort of mystical energy, or perhaps a quantum field connection. However, it is well-known that there are other, non-mystical ways to stimulate these body parts and systems—for example by massage, or via the breath exercises used in both India and China. Whether they are called pranayama or qi gong, these exercises can provide large doses of oxygen the body, so much so that they could produce altered states of consciousness without involving any mystical energies whatsoever. However, ASCs are usually needed to manipulate mystical energies, so this can quickly become a chicken-or-egg dispute.

A Few Words About Auras

Auras are fields of mystical light around people, animals, plants, and sometimes even inanimate objects. Usually they are only seen by psychics, although people suffering from migraine headaches or other neurological difficulties can sometimes see something similar. The basic idea underlying auras is that of the yogic multiple bodies; each body has its own kind of energy and matter, both of which reflect the various planes of existence operating at increasingly higher vibrations. These bodies can separate from the physical body, as in astral projection, thus allowing a person's consciousness to move up through the planes to where they can cohabitate with the creative forces of the universe. Once on a higher plane, its matter and energy can be manipulated and controlled by a trained psychic or magician, and any changes made on the higher planes will affect the matter and energy on the lower planes.

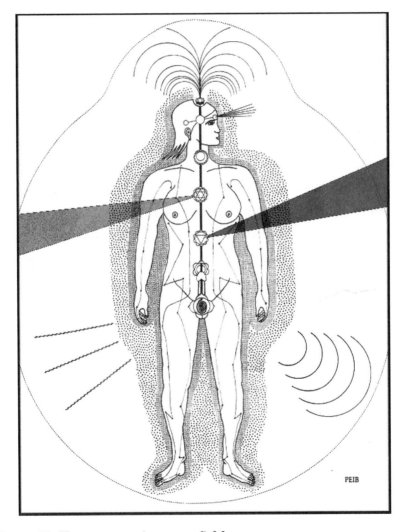

Figure 17: *Human esoteric energy fields.*

A typical listing of the multiple layers, bodies, and/or planes is as follows: etheric, astral, mental, spiritual, and causal. It seems obvious to state that this nomenclature is related to the Vedic system of multiple bodies; unfortunately, however, different metaphysical systems put these terms in different orders, which can be very confusing to students and experts alike. We are inclined to believe that at least some of these bodies, planes, and/or auric layers are as much altered states of consciousness as they are anything physical. They certainly make a useful categorization system for psychics, magicians, mystics, and energy healers.

Figure 17 on page 223, taken from *Real Magic*, shows (1) the traditional Western concepts of the swirling, multilayered human aura; (2) one common arrangement of the Hindu concepts of chakras or psychic centers; (3) the rise of the kundalini serpent through the body in Tantric lore; and (4) a suggestion of a few of the Chinese meridians of qi flow and their associated acupuncture points.

Chapter 9

Energies From Spirits

What *Are* Spirits?

That's a heck of a good question! We wish we had a simple answer for you, but why should the nature of spirits (or vice versa) be any simpler than the nature of quarks or black holes? We live in a complicated multiverse, and some phenomena are so complicated as to demand a multi-model approach. Let's start with Isaac's favorite hobby and look at the word itself, this time by quoting from *Rites of Worship*:

> The word spirit comes from the Latin spiritus, meaning "breathing." The Shorter Oxford English Dictionary defines it as "the animating or life-giving principle in humans and animals," "the immaterial part of a corporeal being, esp. considered as a moral agent; the soul," "immaterial substance, as opp. to body or matter," and "a supernatural, immaterial, rational or intelligent being, usually regarded as imperceptible to humans but capable of becoming visible at will, as an angel, demon, fairy, etc.

usu. with a specifying word." About a dozen or so other meanings, many of them dealing with the authenticity or real nature of a person's feelings or statements are then added. Most of the definitions for "spirit" are also given for "soul," showing the confusion between these two concepts in Western philosophy.[1]

The word spirit comes from "breath," just as the words prana and qi. The definitions of spirit as an energy seem to mirror those of qi, prana, vital force, orgone energy, and so on. Death is often defined as the moment when the spirit departs from a person or animal. We can also define spirit as the non-physical being or beings that inhabit a physical body (or, according to some folks, something generated by the body as a kind of hologram or cybernetic entity). Finally, spirit can be defined as a non-human entity that doesn't have a body, and may never have had one. This can include what traditional cultures may refer to as Elementals, nature spirits, angels, demons, faeries, gods, goddesses, and even Mother Nature herself. All of these can be explained (away) as the archetypes (universal mental constructs) within Jung's collective unconscious, St. Pierre Teilhard De Chardin's noesphere, Isaac's switchboard, or perhaps even the Theosophist's causal plane. In each of these theories, humanity is thought to have a kind of global group-mind. Other explanations offered for spirits contend that they are the aggregation of cultural memories of famous people, the memories of visitors from other planets or dimensions, the infantile memories of seemingly omnipotent parents, the animated and at least marginally self-aware thought-forms created by magicians and mystics, and so on. It would seem that spirits, and thus spiritual energy, could be related to any or all of these disparate ideas.

There are two other concepts that make use of the word "spiritual" that are useful for the reader to be familiar with. First, there's the concept of spiritual hierarchy, or the idea that some spirits are more powerful and important than others. This is very common in the world's religious, magical, and mystical traditions, especially in hierarchical cultures. Then, there's the concept of spiritual warfare, which holds that both physical violence and evil black magic are morally acceptable if done on behalf of your deity, and against the followers of other deities.

For the sake of this book, we are going to assume that spirits are real beings of some sort, whether quasi-physical (made of matter on a higher plane), psychological patterns in individual or collective minds, or energy in some absolute sense that we don't really understand. Personally, we believe that spirits, from the lowliest snail deva to the highest imaginable deities, are at the very least energy patterns (however loosely defined), within and/or accessible to a kind of psychic network that connects all humanity.

Elementals and Nature Spirits

Remember the magical law of personification? The spirits called Elementals are personifications of the four classical Elements. Earth Elementals are usually called gnomes; Water Elementals, undines; Air Elementals, sylphs; and Fire Elementals, salamanders. There are even spirits that are personifications of the Element of Spirit, usually called sprites. While the names of these spirits (except for salamanders) are also the names of other spirits usually thought of as nature spirits, they exist in this classification system primarily as a mental tool for Western ceremonial magicians and mystics, including many Wiccans. They can use these concepts as a way to attain up close and personal relationships with the Four Elements by seeing them as people.[2]

Nature spirits are exactly what they sound like: spirits believed to reside in or near various aspects of nature, such as rocks, streams, hills, trees, oceans, the air, fire, and so on. Nature spirits are part of the worldview of animism (the belief that everything is alive in some sense), as well as animatism (the idea that spirits are what make living things alive). Traditional systems of magic and mysticism in cultures around the globe have all shared these ideas, as can be inferred from our discussion of Taoism and Huna (in these, it is qi and mana that are the animating forces that enables creatures to live). Most modern books about Taoism won't talk much about nature spirits. If you are interested in the Chinese approach, however, look for books on Chinese folk religion (the term snooty anthropologists and theologians use to refer to polytheistic beliefs and practices).

Westerners are far more familiar with the nature spirits from Greek, Roman, and Germanic beliefs, including dryads (tree spirits), naiads (water spirits), nymphs (female spirits of places), satyrs (mountain spirits), fauns (tree spirits), and gnomes, goblins, and dwarves (earth spirits). Some people believe that nature spirits sometimes choose to live in peoples' homes, and become household guardians and helpers, such as the tomtes of Scandinavia and the brownies of Scotland and England.

As we have already seen, animal and plant spirits tend to be personifications of particular species, created by people especially attracted to them, though they can also belong to some of the following categories.

Angels, Demons, and Daemons

Angels and demons are spirits that are said to be messengers of good or evil deities. There are sound arguments to be made that the angels and demons of Zoroastrianism and Judaism were originally deities themselves who were demoted after the triumph of the Zoroastrian priests in Persia and the followers of Jeremiah in Israel. However, angels and demons as they are known in the West today, similar to the good spirits and demons of other cultures, are primarily personifications of various vices and virtues. Those that have centuries of belief to bolster them can exhibit and/or parcel out a fair amount of spiritual energy. In order to share in this energy, however, you will have to play by the theological rules of the religions that invented/discovered them.

Daemons were originally Greek spirits that could be of good, bad, or neutral moral character. Some were seen as sources of inspiration and knowledge, and others as malevolent harbingers and instigators of illness or insanity. Eventually, the word was changed to demon (with a strictly negative connotation) by the early Christians. By the European Middle Ages, only ceremonial magicians remembered the original neutral and positive versions of the concept. Such magicians would perform rituals in which they would summon or evoke a daemon or daemons into magical triangles while staying safely within magical circles, and then attempt to force, bribe, or cajole information from the supposedly trapped daemon or daemons. Hostile observers referred to this process as demon worship, and many a ceremonial magician had to be fast on his feet or quick with his wits to escape persecution for "consorting with evil spirits." Some modern magicians claim that an angel or daemon can be created by a magician as a sort of psychic robot that will perform various magical services for its creators.

Many people are terrified of demons, and think that if they practice any sort of magical or mystical system that isn't mainstream or generally accepted, or if they go traveling on astral planes, then horrible demons will be everywhere. We suggest that you think of demons as psychic predators. Just as lions, rattlesnakes, and wolves are usually comparatively rare in their territories, compared to the number of other animals, so are demons in the Otherworld's landscape—and they are as likely to be afraid of you as you are of them.

Faeries, Fairies, and Aliens

The faerie folk deserve a book unto themselves, and indeed there are many such texts. They appear all around the world in most cultures with remarkably similar characteristics. In Ireland they are known as the *sidhe*, in Scandinavia as elves, in Japan as *yokai*, and in England as faeries. Usually they are said to live in the Otherworld, a parallel dimension that overlaps earthly reality and from which they can appear, especially under certain magical circumstances, to interact with humans. Sometimes they are beautiful and attractive, sometimes hideous and frightening, and sometimes they may appear as an animal (such as a fox in Japan) or a human.

There exist certain traditions—those in Irish mythology, for example—that the faeries are actually old gods and goddesses who have lost their mortal worshipers and been replaced by the deities of new peoples. In *The Book of Conquests*, there are explicit narratives that tell of one group of supernatural beings being conquered by another and having to move into the sidhe mounds (the burial mounds of Neolithic Irish peoples), only to be joined by their onetime conquerors when yet another super-natural migration occured.

In many of these tales, the interests and motivations of faeries often seem to be alien and incomprehensible to their mere mortal counterparts. Their fondness for kidnapping people (especially children), their magical powers, the way they seem to bend time, and the way they alter the memories of those they take into their realm have led a number of researchers to suggest that faeries may have something to do with extraterrestrials and their antisocial behavior. Don't laugh—in his classic book, *Cosmic Trigger I*, Robert Anton Wilson suggested some 30 years ago that beliefs regarding faeries and aliens might actually point to something else entirely: an otherworldly being that is neither. Of course, if these faeries/aliens were in fact remnant godlings from Neolithic peoples, this would explain their incomprehensible otherness; certainly, their actions would not make sense to modern peoples.

On the other paw, the cute little winged people that most people think of when they hear or read the word fairy, are probably the result of the honorific diminutives that were once used to refer to the faeries. Monikers such as "the gentry," "the good people," "the darling little ones," and so on were used to reassure any listening faeries that they were loved and respected. After a while, the idea of the faery unified with the idea of the local nature or household spirit, which was often perceived as a small creature as well. However, because so many people today believe in the Tinkerbell version of faeries, perhaps the little ones now exist as spirits created by humans. If so, Isaac prefers to refer to these as fairies, rather than faeries.

In any event, we advise against messing with faeries unless you know what you are doing and have studied your folklore well. Faerie energies are so difficult to control and are so, well, alien, that most modern mystics and magicians would be better off just leaving them alone.[3] If you want to put out a plate of milk and cookies for the "little people," that's okay—it might even bring you good luck (as long as you never forget to replenish the goodies). On the other hand, if you are ever abducted by an alien, you might want to choose to see it as one of the gentry, which may encourage it to change its appearance and behavior to match the folktales. Most importantly, don't eat or drink anything while you're in the Otherworld!

Ancestors, the Mighty Dead, and Other Ghosts

Death is nature's way of telling you to slow down. Altered states of consciousness usually alter one's sense of time as well as other perceptions. Perhaps the so-called afterlife is merely a prolonged near-death experience (NDE). Research in the field of NDEs indicates striking similarities in subjects' NDE narratives, and specific patterns in these narratives that seem to match personal belief systems (for example, the presence of a heaven and/or hell for the Christian or the Buddhist). After you are greeted on the other side, will you experience merely what you expect to happen? If so, the idea of having someone read to you from a *Book of the Dead* (a series of instructions, sort of an afterlife travel guide, if you will) as you die in order to prepare you seems pretty sensible to us. After all, it couldn't hurt!

Most scientific evidence for the survival of the soul and/or reincarnation is shaky at best, and people who research the topic are rarely unbiased. Spiritualist narratives and folk tales about reincarnation reveal a partial survival of personality at best, which fits in well with Isaac's theory of the switchboard. Pure, classic, reincarnation theory indicates that only the *atman* or *monad* (the spark of divine fire) survives, and without specific memories—just tendencies or inclinations to be carried forward into the next life.

However, while the evidence for survival after death is all circumstantial, it is also quite substantial. Most cultures engage in ancestor worship practices, at least in the sense of showing honor and respect towards one's ancestors. Setting up an ancestor shrine in your home and stopping there to honor them regularly (and thus giving them your personal mystical energies) is an excellent way to prepare yourself to receive whatever energies they may have to give you in return. Your ancestor shrine may be a wide shelf or a shallow box hung against a wall. It should be decorated with photos, drawings, statues, or other items that remind you of your ancestors and your ethnic heritages, whatever they may be. Do some genealogical research; write an ancestor invocation listing as many of their names as you can. An ancestor altar should have a votive or seven-day candle burning most of the time, and you should try to spend at least 10 minutes a day communing with your ancestral spirits. You will find that when your ancestors seem more like friendly spirits that you expect to join someday, you will no longer fear death but see it as a new adventure.

Of course, not all deceased people are ancestors. Some die without having children, and some die under circumstances in which they weren't really "all there" anymore. As most of the world's traditions on the topic would have it, ghosts (from the German *geist*, meaning "spirit") are the spirits of dead people or other animals; they can be friendly (rare), hungry for human energies (also rare), hostile (common), or indifferent (the vast majority). Isaac believes, as do some other psychic researchers, that ghosts who appear to haunt particular locations, supposedly as a result of a sad or violent death, in fact are not deceased human spirits in the usual sense at all. He believes they are psychic videotapes created by a mystically charged event, and occurring at a location where there is enough mystical energy to take the shape of that event—much as a mystic or a magician may shape her or his own mystical energies (or astral matter) to create an energy field to perform a spell or some other energy working.

The single most confusing and annoying characteristic of most mystical energies is that they change themselves to fit the intentions, hopes, or fears of the observer. If you are fearful that your dead Aunt Petunia always hated you and wanted to harm you, then any spiritual energies you encounter that resemble her in any way may be shaped by your subconscious projections into a hostile "ghost" that actually isn't her spirit at all, but your own paranoia taking form. In other words, the ghost becomes the projection of your inner mental life onto the external world. We could call such energy entities faux ghosts, we suppose (and any faux news you received from them would, of course, have to be taken with many grains of salt).

Another category of deceased human spirit is that of the mighty dead. These are spirits that have been created by people honoring a famous real or mythical person, and telling stories about him or her for generations. Thus, one gets great Caesar's ghost; or the ghost of George Washington; or that of Cuchullain, the legendary Irish hero; or El Cid; or Pecos Bill; or some other superman or superwoman. At this point we begin to touch the edges of what Taylor Ellwood and Storm Constantine[4] call "pop-culture magick," in their excellent book of that name.

In order to understand this phenomenon, it might be helpful to recall that attention directs energy. Historical heroes, famous warriors, breakthrough scientists, rock stars, and even brilliantly conceived and portrayed fictional characters can all become archetypes, or circuits in the switchboard, if you prefer. If they are thought of as real people (even if they are not), there will be a lot of attention, and hence energy, attached to their personages. With that attention follows magical and/or spiritual energies, charging up the mental images in the same way that some deities may have been created by humans. Why do you think there are so many people who literally worship Elvis or Princess Diana or Xena? They aren't just worshiping (giving energy to) departed souls; they are worshiping the *ideas* of them.

Devas and Deities

Deva is a Sanskrit word that refers to a deity, demigod, or other powerful spirit of a benign nature. To some of the Theosophists, devas were the major "angelic" forces behind nature.[5] In the concept best known to New Agers and Neo-Pagans, devas are spirits that represent the mystical energy of plants. This idea was made famous by the work of the Findhorn Community in Scotland,[6] which supposedly managed to grow giant vegetables by contacting the devas of the plants through resident mediums.

While New Agers were approaching devas through Spiritualism and Theosophy in the 1960s, elsewhere hippies were learning from Native Americans about the powerful effects of psychedelic herbs, mushrooms, and cacti. It turned out that many who consumed peyote buttons reported having very similar visions of a vegetation spirit known as San Mescalito. This was about the time Carlos Castenada was writing his novels about a

Native American shaman named Don Juan, who in these stories spoke a great deal about so-called spirit allies that appeared in the form of animals and helped shamans do their energy workings. A few years later, Oberon and Morning Glory Zell-Ravenheart discovered that people using the belladonna plant for trances reported seeing the same pale "Fair Lady," whom they believed to be the spirit of the plant.

These concepts have merged together over the last few decades to create the idea that there are spiritual beings that are personifications of particular plant and animal species. Whether every species gets one or not is unclear, although it seems that only the psychedelic plant species and the attractive and/or powerful animal species get much publicity today. It may very well be that people who munch peyote or belladonna (neither one is recommended!) are connecting to the same parts of the collective unconscious or the global group-mind. If so, it's possible that they could have visions of the same archetypes. If this has been going on for centuries or even millennia, it could build up a pretty good charge to a spirit.

The thing about visions, of course, is that they are only rarely shared. The psychedelic plants might have an advantage here, but each person's vision of the spirit of the Bear, or the Horse, or the Hawk, or any other species-specific deva or "ally," will probably be quite different in its specifics, and will depend in large part on how much each person actually knows about the behavior and characteristics of the species. Hence, we have a bit of skepticism about animal devas, unless they are in fact gods and godlings (minor or local gods) created by previous generations of people who lived with the species and knew them well. In that case, devas might be real, but the clarity or reliability of any given would-be shaman's vision would be suspect at best.

As for deities in general, gods and goddesses may be all of the possible examples we mentioned at the beginning of this chapter—powerful spiritual beings, archetypes, memories of famous people, and so on. We're willing to consider that they are people with more advanced knowledge and awareness than we have, and who aren't burdened with physical bodies unless they want them. We're even willing to entertain the possibility that each one might be a particular aspect, emanation, or face of the Goddess and the God, Shakti and Shiva, yin and yang. Or they might be wholly imaginary—but we don't care! Believing in the deities, or any of the other spirits we've talked about in this book, makes our lives richer and more meaningful. It also gives our efforts to produce magical or psychic phenomena a real boost when we need it, thus producing "coincidences" over and over again.

When you contact a deity or other spirit, you don't usually hear words, and only rarely will you receive a vision. What you usually get is feelings—quiet or overwhelming emotions, electricity going up your spine, the hair on the top of your head standing up, or strength filling you up. Sometimes you get flashes of images, smells from nowhere, music or other sounds. Sometimes you receive unutterable peace and tranquility. What we do know as clergy and magicians is that all of these permutations of spiritual energy can strengthen and focus whatever magical, mystical, psychic, artistic, or erotic work we wish to achieve. And we thank the gods and goddesses for that!

Gaia and the Supreme Being

Do you remember Francis Barrett saying that "stones inherit great virtues, which they receive through the spheres and activity of the celestial influences, by the medium of the soul or spirit of the world"? Was he thinking of Gaia when he wrote this? Gaia is the now-popular name for what previous generations of people have called Mother Nature and the Earth Mother, among others. In 1970, Oberon Zell-Ravenheart (then just Tim Zell) published a Neo-Pagan essay about what would come to be known as the "Gaea Thesis," which states that the Earth Mother is a living being composed of the Earth's entire biosphere. He wrote this four years before James Lovelock published his "Gaia Hypothesis."

In the same year that Lovelock published, Isaac wrote an essay titled "What Do Druids Believe?" This has since been published many times in newsletters, books, and on the authors' Website. Isaac had this to say about Gaia/Gaea:

> It is necessary to respect and love Nature as divine in Her own right, and to accept ourselves as part of Nature and not Her "rulers." Many accept "the Gaia theory" that the earth's entire biosphere can be usefully seen as a single living "super being" on multiple levels of reality—rocks as Her bones, the oceans and atmosphere as Her circulatory system, plants and fungi as Her skin, and so forth, all tied into an infinitely complex network of feedback systems. Such metaphors are useful in geology, biology, atmospheric and oceanic sciences, and ecology. We humans are Her children, but so are all other living beings, and any special privileges we might have are balanced by equal responsibilities. As the one super

being that every human lives within, and without whom we would all die, Mother Nature is worthy of that respect called "worship," for we recognize Her worth.[7]

Isaac has been a priest of the Earth Mother since 1969, leading public worship of her, and making sacrifices both pleasant and sappy. It has been his experience that the Earth as a whole is a living, sentient being, and that the Chinese idea of terrestrial qi is, if anything, understated. Perhaps Gaia doesn't need human worship in the same way that lesser deities might in order to replenish their energies, but *Gaia needs us to experience worshiping her*—that is to say, to experience showing her the respect and attention she needs and deserves, before we mortals drag her back to one-celled organisms and oily oceans again.

Much of what we have already stated about working with nature spirits is directly applicable to working with Gaia— after all, she's our Mother! Go to places of natural beauty and look for her. You will find her "in the softness of a kitten and the coolness of a lake, in the sweetness of honey and the savor of fruits."[8] And if you come to her with love, courage, and determination in your heart, she will bless you with spiritual abundance.

Now about that Supreme Being. We're actually not going to say a lot about him/her/it/them. The topic is too big for this book, or any other; furthermore, all of the anthropomorphic (human-like) versions that have been offered throughout history have caused far more misery than benefit to our species. But here's an option for those of you who believe that you are contacting, and receiving blessing from, a Supreme Being, and it's one many of you may already follow: just open yourself to the energies that underlie all reality, understanding that anything big enough to create billions of galaxies, each with billions of stars and at least hundreds of millions of planets with life, probably doesn't look like a Middle Eastern man. You can call it God, and others can call it qi, the spiritual or causal plane, the universal quantum field, the Tao, or the Force.

Chapter 10

Generating and Focusing Mystical Energies

An Overview

Whether you are thinking in terms of qi, psi, prana, orgone, or spiritual energies, there are many different ways to generate mystical energies and focus them for a particular purpose. Isaac's other books will be useful for the reader who wants to go into this topic in depth, but for now we'll just touch on the highlights. Each method has its own benefits and drawbacks, and will work well for some people and not others, and in different places and circumstances. But first, an important warning: Don't think that you are generating or controlling energy when all you are doing is feeling energy. As we would hope this book has made clear so far, there are many different kinds of energy (both mystical and mundane) that humans are capable of sensing and interacting with, either directly or indirectly. Many people confuse any energy with effective energy, and any change in their state of consciousness with an appropriate state change.

Why would people who have little idea of what they are doing be happy even when the experienced energy workers observing them are banging their heads against the nearest tree in frustration? Because most methods for generating or tapping into mystical energies also stimulate the production of endorphins—the brain chemicals that suppress pain and make people feel good. But just feeling good isn't enough. A would-be energy worker of any variety needs to pay attention to both the quantity and the quality of the mystical energies he or she is generating, as well as use the appropriate techniques to focus and use them effectively.

One way to think of the process of generating energies is to imagine that your body is a mystical or biochemical generator revving up to produce energy flows. The Hindu practice of pranayama, as well as many qi gong exercises, can produce such bodily changes as elevated temperature, biochemical reactions in the digestive tract, and alterations in oxygen levels in the brain. Oftentimes, novices will interpret these physical changes as evidence of the increased flow of mystical energies within their bodies. Indeed, most of the energy-generating techniques we will look at in this chapter can produce sensations of increased mystical energies.

Isaac noted many years ago in *Real Magic* that anything that gets a person excited seems to be able to change their psychic energy levels as well. Therefore, we're not going to be able to draw a sharp line here between genuine and illusory perceptions of mystical energies. For centuries, mystical teachers have agreed that the ability to know the difference takes lots of practice, and that, in the long run, the proof is in the results.

Visual Methods

Because humans are primarily a visual species, it should be no surprise that drawings, paintings, carvings, sculptures (and in modern times, photographs) have been and are still used in many magical, mystical, and mundane energy systems to arouse human emotions and generate mystical energies. These kinds of representations are very useful for focusing attention during a spiritual invocation or magical spell, as the ancient cave shamans may have known when they painted pictures of humans hunting bison, reindeer, or mammoths so long ago.

Certainly, visual representations, such as the mandalas of Hindus and Buddhists, the magical sigils of Western ceremonial magicians, the sand paintings of the Southwestern Native Americans, and the icons of the Eastern Orthodox Catholics, are powerful tools that generate energies even during the process of their creation—a task that can, in some cases, take not just hours but days to complete. The more complex these images are, the more precisely their users can focus their attention on the target and goal of an energy working, whether it is a blessing, a healing, or an exorcism. The special symbols used by reiki masters serve both as triggering images to enable the energy worker to channel the reiki energy, and as focusing tools to control the exact "flavor" of reiki energy being used.

Auditory Methods

While there is very little written in mystical and magical literature about the psychic effects of sheer beauty, certainly creators and performers in all genres of art know how magical a superb performance or production of a work of art can be. Arguably, the second most important sense in humans is hearing; therefore, music, singing, and chanting are also excellent means of generating and focusing mystical energies.

Whether speaking or singing mantras from India, uttering incantations from the *Key of Solomon* (a book on magic attributed to King Solomon), or speaking invocations to a chosen deity, both the meaning and the sounds of the words chosen are important—hence the magical law of words of power. In these contexts, the intellectual and emotional meanings of words are equally important (though many writers on mystical matters tend to emphasize one over the other), as is the aesthetic quality of the sounds. When mantras, chants, or songs are performed in ways that accentuate or heighten the physical vibrations caused in the chanters and/or listeners (such as in the use of drums or gongs), sounds turn into movement. Thus, the auditory becomes kinesthetic.

Kinesthetic Methods

People have always used dancing, running, spinning, and other vigorous physical activities as ways to enter into altered states of consciousness and generate mystical energies. Qi gong and t'ai chi, for example, are primarily kinesthetic methods, meant to generate qi within the body and open the practitioner to the flow of qi from terrestrial and celestial sources.

Dancing can be quite effective in the generation of mystical energies, but, as with any art form, it requires study and practice in order to gain the maximum benefit. For example, if you wish to "trance-dance" with others, you should acquaint yourself fully with the technique and the art, so that everyone participating can have the best possible experience. The amount of mystical energies created by a room full of whirling Sufi dancers, Santeria worshippers, or even country or ballroom dancers can be amazing (although the first two groups are likely to be the most adept at applying the energies generated to mystical purposes). As Isaac said in *Rites of Worship*:

Mystical energies stimulate mystical energies—the more you generate, the more you attract, and vice versa. Rhythmic sounds and actions can control these feedback loops, altering the strength and speed of the buildup, as well as focusing the consciousness of each participant. A concert is a good secular place to see such mystical energy feedback loops. If the artists are truly talented, there is a palpable energy exchange between the audience and the performers. Expert performers learn to shape the feedback loops to produce the total artistic effect they want.[1]

A drum circle under the stars, with dancers and drummers communicating with motion and sound, can generate life-changing trances and powerful magic!

Erotic Methods

If there is one thing that (good) sex is, it's exciting! Ergo, it should be capable of generating mystical energies. Almost anyone, no matter how incompetent, will find him- or herself charged up and glowing, on more than one level of reality, after a passionate interlude. This is why almost every mystical and magical tradition in the world has some form of often secret erotic mysticism or sex magic as part of its system.

Many readers of this book will have already heard of Tantra, a magical/mystical tradition in both Hinduism and Buddhism that shocked—shocked, we say!—Madame Blavatsky and the other early leaders of Theosophy. Thanks primarily to their writings, most Westerners for the last hundred years or so have assumed that Tantra was some form of a degenerate "left-hand path" or evil black magic. Tantra *was* referred to by some folks in India as a left-hand path, but that phrase was originally used to denote a path of enlightenment that was sensualist rather than ascetic. The original Tantric practitioners felt that the way to get rid of attachments to the material world was to over-indulge in all of them (not just the sexual ones), rather than avoiding them. It was the puritanism of the early Theosophists, and their ignorance of the sex-magic traditions in Rosicrucianism, alchemy, and the European Paleo-Pagan cultures that led them to assume that the Dionysian paths were wicked and the Apollonian ones were virtuous.

That said, because sex is such a powerful physical and psychological activity, serious practitioners of erotic mysticism and magic, whether in India, China, Scandinavia, Greece, Rome, Africa, or anywhere else, were careful not to do what they did out in the middle of the street (after all, they didn't want to scare any horses), except during specific holidays when risqué behavior and downright debauchery were considered acceptable. Whether you are talking about prana, qi, mana, or any other variant of mystical energy that affects people, you can do interesting things with sexually generated energies.

In the kundalini yoga practiced by the Tantrics in India, for example, *yabyum*, or ritual sexual intercourse between highly trained participants, was used to arouse the sleeping kundalini serpent in the root chakra and send it up the sushumna channel and out of the top of the participants' heads—thus inducing an ecstatic state, often experienced as oneness with a divinity. Because the partners in each couple performing yabyum were expected to perceive the other as Shiva or Shakti while arousing the serpent, it could be said that physical union with the divine led to spiritual union with the divine.

What actually happens during a kundalini rising? One way to describe it is that one's conscious attention is exquisitely focused on one chakra after another, stimulating the muscles, nerves, and glands near each, and moving all the way up to one's brain. Most people who have had this happen to them describe it as a bolt of electricity or an explosion of fire sweeping up their bodies and out into space. Even if there were no mystical organs in the human body, such an experience is bound to generate a lot of prana! In Tantra, this prana is supposed to be used for theurgical purposes—to attain union with a deity, give that deity extra prana, and receive spiritual enlightenment.

In Chinese sexual alchemy—as it is in Western alchemy's hidden eroticism and Western sex magic traditions—the qi or life force is generated through various sexual activities, and is then focused and directed for both thaumaturgical and theurgical purposes (usually pertaining to sexuality or fertility). There are many books available that purport to instruct the reader in these various techniques. As much as your humble authors approve of sex in most of its many delightful forms, we do feel it incumbent upon us to issue a warning:[2] Safe, ethical, and effective use of sex as a source of mystical energies for spiritual, magical, artistic, or healing purposes—whether alone, in a duo, or in a group—requires that all the participants be mature, well-balanced, self-confident, and self-disciplined individuals who share the same erotic preferences, are willing to take directions, and who limit their sexual activities to within the group. Unfortunately, Western culture is so schizophrenic about sexuality that using sex to raise mystical energies is something best kept behind closed doors and among consenting adults—at least for the next hundred years or so.

Biochemical Methods

Certain beverages, herbs, cactus buttons, funny mushrooms, and modern pharmaceutical substances—all of which count as drugs—can cause their users to generate enormous amounts of emotional and mystical energies and/or open them up to a potent flux of mystical energies, spiritual contacts, and psychic experiences. This is not always A Good Thing. The way the brain organizes incoming information is usually distorted and confused by drugs, which can make it difficult for the user to focus on the original intention of the energy working. If you use such substances, you can wind up generating or tapping into the wrong variety of mystical energy—or conversely, have the right sort rush through your system so powerfully that it damages your mystical channels. The perception of reality can shift so drastically that the magician or mystic who uses drugs may wind up doing serious damage to him- or herself on multiple levels of reality.

While Aleister Crowley performed many experiments with the drugs available to him at the turn of the previous century—some for magical or mystical purposes, and some just for fun—and kept incredibly detailed journals of the results, by and large drugs are a poor tool, especially for anyone who lacks proper guidance and training and has no one to baby-sit while his or her consciousness goes off to Alpha Centauri or Sirius. It should also be noted that only a few drugs are legal in most of the world today—and even those that are legal have many strictures guiding and regulating their use. These include tobacco, caffeine, alcohol (unless you are in a Muslim nation), and legally prescribed medications—not all of which are suitable for use in magical or mystical energy workings, although the use of wine, beer, or ale is common in the West (as is tobacco among the Wannabe Indian tribe).

Mental Methods

It's difficult to generate mystical energies just by thinking about them. If you have meditated a lot about prana or qi or other mystical energies, and accumulated a collection of mental cues to remind you of past energy experiences, then concentration, contemplation, and meditation may be used to trigger those memories, which may in turn generate similar energies. This takes time, though an experienced meditator can often tap into significant quantities of mystical energies. Meditation and concentration do provide an advantage for the energy worker in that they allow him or her to clarify and fine tune the content of their working—and hopefully, repeat the process over and over again.

Spiritual Methods

The term spiritual, similar to spirit, has many meanings. For some people it's a synonym for religious, and implies membership in a particular religion, sect, denomination, or cult. Others, however, insist on distinguishing religion from spirituality; for them, the word spiritual denotes personal meditation, mysticism, and/or magical activity. For yet others, it implies piety or virtue, or a rejection of the material world. In this section, we are going to focus on the oldest meaning of the word, one that implies interactions with spirits (however these are defined).

Different sorts of spirits can be contacted and persuaded (or they can volunteer) to give the mystic, the magician, or any other energy worker anywhere from a little to a great deal of mystical energies. This can take the form of inspiration by the spirit, conversation between the spirit and the worker, a channeling of words or mystical energies from the spirit through the worker, or even the possession of the energy worker by the spirit.

When this contact and interaction unfolds more or less as you had hoped, the process can be considered a form of tapping the spirit for mystical energies and data. Sometimes, however, the spirit seems to be more in charge of the situation than the magician or mystic is, leading to old cautionary tales about not biting off more than you can chew.

So how does one persuade spirits to grant their energies to fulfill your needs? The traditional methods include prayers, invocations ("callings-in"), evocations ("callings-out"), and making gifts or sacrifices (literal or metaphorical). It has only been during the last 100 years or so that people have invented methods of magic and mysticism that did not involve the activity of spirits. However, all of these methods may be used with any of the techniques we've been discussing in this chapter in order to get a spirit's attention and focus your mind on what you're doing.

The most common method of contacting spirits that are considered to be superior (such as ancestors or deities) is through private or public worship, which has nothing to do with groveling, and everything to do with showing love and respect. All of the methods of generating and focusing mystical energies—visual, auditory, kinesthetic, and so on—can be used to create powerful and effective worship experiences.[3] These will often, though not always, take the form of rituals—a somewhat scary word that merely means an ordered sequence of events (think of a recipe or a computer program) designed to produce predictable results.

Tapping Into Mystical Energies

Tapping into mystical energies involves opening ourselves up to their presence, making a psychic, magical, and/or spiritual connection to them, and then pulling or receiving the mystical energies into ourselves for theurgical or thaumaturgical purposes. Isaac originally coined the term "tapping" as a metaphor to describe the process of drawing out these energies, taken from tapping into a keg of beer. "Channeling" can be seen as more passive way of accomplishing the same effects simply by opening yourself up to mystical energies that will easily flow into you when you are relaxed. Channeling is best known these days as a New Age substitution for the old Spiritualist term mediumship, and there are some who still use it in that sense exclusively for channeling spiritual energies. However, based on what we know about qi gong and t'ai chi, it seems clear that one major category of mystical energies—qi—is ready to flow into you as soon as you open and clear your mystical channels. Tapping into a keg of good, dark stout can be a matter of either opening a spigot and letting gravity fill your glass, or using a pressurized gadget of some sort to pump the stout upstairs to the pub. So, perhaps some channeling can be likened to the former method. For the purposes of this book, we will define tapping and channeling as two ways to receive mystical energies from various sources, including the universe in general, the Earth, the ether, energetically charged objects, and people, animals, and/or spirits.

As we've discussed throughout this book, many systems of mysticism and magic believe that the universe is filled with mystical energies, whether they call those energies qi, prana, psi, vril, or the Force. (Don't laugh—after all, "it surrounds us, it penetrates us, it binds the galaxy together!"[4]) Many energy-working systems talk about pulling mystical energies from the ether or etheric plane, or from the air surrounding places of natural beauty, as Isaac pointed out in *Rites of Worship*:

In fact, it's the presence of such mystical energies that makes many people want to treat these spots reverently, and which causes them to be turned into parks and preserves. When you are at Niagara Falls, Old Faithful geyser in Yellowstone National Park, Mont St. Michael's, an ocean beach, or outside during a thunderstorm or hurricane, the energy of the moving air and/or water seems to generate even more mystical energies than those present at the quieter and less dramatic power spots. Places that have been used for many years as ceremonial sites often have strong mystical energies stored within them, especially if artificial changes have been made to the land, such as the building of stone circles or pyramids. In general, the age of the site in its current form, the number of living plants and animals present, the amount of kinetic energy there, and the history of its use for magical/spiritual purposes, seem to be the major variables determining the quantity of mystical energies available.[5]

All of this matches what the Chinese mystics say to us about celestial-, terrestrial-, and weather-related qi. Nature is full of mystical power for those who are sensitive to its ebbs and flows.

How much mystical energy you can tap into from ceremonial tools or other objects depends on the age of the object and whether it has been charged up with mystical energies on multiple occasions. Most mystics using such tools will use them as symbols to help them tap into mystical energies through them. Icons, idols, and other artistic depictions of spirits, because of the magical law of similarity, are especially popular ceremonial objects.

Group Energy-Working

Whether they are families, employees in workplaces, military units, church congregations, or healing circles, groups have their own kinds of energy. Patterns of overlapping physical, psychological, and social connections can allow mystical energies to build on each other and create the most powerful psychic, magical, and mystical fields possible. Just as with every other form of energy, you can learn to notice ebbs and flows of the non-mystical energies, and in time you will learn how they effect your attempts to use the mystical ones.

Tapping into or channeling energies from other people is part of why group rituals—when done well—can be so effective. The creation of a group mind enables the participants to share their mystical energies with each other and remain focused on a particular thaumaturgical or theurgical target and goal. A group mind is easier to create when the members share many different connections—hence the popularity of company or union sporting leagues, church dance clubs, and study groups working within a particular mystical tradition. The more time people spend with each other, the better their group mind will be.

Of course, if your group is performing mystical exercises together, the group mind they create (consciously or not) can become very powerful. That's why all over East Asia you can find crowds of hundreds of people (adding up to hundreds of millions) doing t'ai chi together, and all over the Islamic world you can see crowds of men doing their prayers together five times a day, knowing that hundreds of millions of others are doing the same thing. On special days of the year, literally billions of people create group minds to celebrate Easter or Halloween, or the many combined holidays of Hannakwayulmas that fall in December. With practice you can learn to tap into the mystical energies being generated by the local and global group minds on these special occasions.

Chapter 11

A Few Conclusions

We've looked at a lot of different kinds of energy in this book. Trying to sum up everything is a bit of a daunting task, so we're going to organize everything into a chart representing our current assessments (as of early 2007). The first column in Table 15 lists the names and subcategories of the different mystical energies we've discussed. The second column indicates whether each kind of energy seems to be universally distributed, or "cosmic." The third column shows whether each kind of energy is connected to a life force of some sort. The fourth column indicates whether each kind of energy might be connected to other, already known energies (for example, energies that are entirely or primarily life force energies would all have connections to biochemical or neural energy). The fifth column shows our guesses as to whether each energy type represents a kind of relationship, whether it be one of conscious association, psychological influence, perception, the product of other energies interacting, or even quantum entanglement. The last column lists any additional notes we felt it would be prudent to add.

Energy Type	Cosmic Energy	Life Energy	Connected to Mundane Energies?	Works via Relationship?	Notes
Spirits	Y	N	N	Y	May be psi or mana fields
Elemental	N	N	N	Y	Mostly association
Natural Mana	Y	Y	Y	N	
Animal Mana	N	Y	Y	N	
Psychic or Magical Mana	N	N	Y	Y	See psi
Odic Force	N	Y	M	?	
Vril	Y	Y	Y	Y	Fictional
Ectoplasm	N	Y	Y	N	Possibly fictional
Orgone	Y	Y	Y	?	Life force
Animal Magnetism	N	Y	Y	?	Life force
Etheric	Y	Y	Y	?	Theosophical planes
Astral	Y	N	N	?	Theosophical planes
Mental	Y	N	N	Y	Theosophical planes
Causal	Y	N	Y	Y	Theosophical planes
Psi, ESP	?	N	?	Y	Passive

Table 15: *Possible conclusions regarding mystical energies.*

Energy Type	Cosmic Energy	Life Energy	Connected to Mundane Energies?	Works via Relationship?	Notes
Psi, Hypercognition	?	N	?	Y	Passive
Psi, PK	?	N	Y	Y	Active
Psi, Antipsi	?	N	Y	?	Mixed
Solar	N	N	Y	Y	Seasonal/ cyclical
Lunar	N	N	Y	Y	Cyclical
Astrological	Y	N	?	Y	Possibly cyclical
Ley Line	N	N	M	M	Possibly fictional
Plant	N	N	Y	Y	
Animal	N	N	N	Y	
Crystal	N	N	N	Y	Mostly imaginary
Celestial Qi	Y	M	Y	?	
Animal Qi	N	Y	Y	?	Life force
Terrestrial Qi	Y	N	Y	?	
Kundalini	N	Y	Y	?	Biochemical and neural
Chakra	N	Y	Y	M	Biochemical and neural
Prana	N	Y	Y	N	Biochemical and neural
The Force	Y	Y	M	Y	Fictional

Table 15: *Possible conclusions regarding mystical energies. (Continued)*

Several philosophies contend that life force energies are universally distributed, but there's no known life on the moon, so this may be an overstatement, or the systems may conceive of atmospheric or terrestrial distribution as being universal. In the chart, Y equals yes, N equals no, M equals maybe, and ? means that we just don't know. As the chart shows, there's a lot we don't know.

Yet the chart also shows some interesting patterns. It seems to us that the various mystical energy systems humans have invented have been attempts to explain subconsciously perceived energy fields and flows. Perhaps the various cosmic energies might be a part of what the physicists are calling dark energy— which may or may not be a function of dark matter. We know that dark matter and energy interact with the readily perceivable forms of matter and energy; so do the cosmic kinds of mystical energy.

The life force energies may be energy fields and flows generated by organic molecules and structures, such as the neural energy generated by brain cells. Dark matter and energy quantum fields may play a role as well, thus blurring the distinctions between cosmic and life energies.

Some forms of mystical energy, such as the plant and animal powers, as well as some of the solar, lunar, and astrological influences, may be primarily psychological functions that affect our emotions and imaginations, thus exciting or depressing our biochemical energies and affecting all of the other energies, mundane or mystical, that are connected to the human body.

The various planes of the Theosophists and other New Agers may be partly the perception of cosmic mystical energies, and partly the states of consciousness in which you can perceive some of the otherwise invisible energies in the multiverse. The idea that matter vibrates faster on the higher planes than it does on the lower ones may be an extension of the four states of physical matter (solid, liquid, gas, and plasma equal the classical four Elements?). However, this doesn't play out logically when you remember that people on the astral plane think of themselves as having astral bodies that can pass through mundane matter. If a bunch of air can't go through steel easily,[1] how could an astral body? Back in 1970, Isaac suggested that astral bodies are hallucinations generated by insecure people doing what parapsychologists call remote viewing or traveling clairvoyance. This still seems plausible, so all the trance work done by Theosophists, hermeticists, and ceremonial magicians on the higher planes may simply be comfortable altered states of consciousness.

Psi is the real puzzle, one that may be solved by examining the psychic talents in their subcategories. We think that extrasensory perception and hypercognition may involve perceiving entangled connections in several of the universally distributed quantum fields, in which case psi is not an energy per se, but a relationship to the multiverse. On the other paw, all the forms of psychokinesis involve interactions with that same multiverse on a physical level; therefore, psi is probably one or more kinds of energy, because it takes energy to affect energy.

The anti-psi powers are a mixed bag. Perhaps the ones that affect thoughts (such as catapsi, negapsi, and so on) are more similar to ESP and hypercognition, and thus are relationships and perceptions rather than energies, while the ones that affect power levels seem more like PK. All of the antipsi powers seem to involve generating or altering energy fields and flows, with subsequent effects on the information being transmitted and/or perceived. Could they all involve psi as an energy? We don't know.

Perhaps that's the real message of this book. There is so much that we just don't know about the multiverse in which we live. Keeping an open mind (but not an empty head) is essential to increasing our understanding. We know the danger that anything unknown can become a target of human projections. Therefore we hesitate to state flatly that, as scientists learn more about the nature of dark matter and energy and the quantum fields within living beings, we will find out more about the strange energies we've been discussing in this book, or increase our understanding of psychic, magical, and spiritual phenomena. But that's where we're placing our bets.

Appendix A

Additional Reading

The following titles are likely to be of interest and value to the reader, especially if she or he is a beginner in these fields.

Adler, Margot. *Drawing Down the Moon*. New York: Penguin Books, 2006.

Bonewits, Isaac. *Bonewits's Essential Guide to Witchcraft and Wicca*. New York: Citadel, 2006.

———. *Bonewits's Essential Guide to Druidism*. New York: Citadel, 2006.

Cramer, Diane L. *How to Give an Astrological Health Reading*. Tempe, Ariz.: American Federation of Astrologers, 1996.

Dennis, Johnnie T. *The Complete Idiot's Guide to Physics*. New York: Alpha Books, 2003.

Douglas, Bill. *The Complete Idiot's Guide to T'ai Chi and Qi Dong*. New York: Alpha Books, 2005.

Eliade, Mircea. *Shamanism*. Princeton, NJ: Princeton University Press, 1972.

———. *A History of Religious Ideas, Vol. 1—From the Stone Age to the Eleusinian Mysteries*. Chicago, Ill.: University of Chicago Press, 1981.

———. *A History of Religious Ideas, Vol. 2—From Gautama Buddha to the Triumph of Christianity*. Chicago, Ill.: University of Chicago Press, 1985.

Ellwood, Taylor and Storm Constantine. *Pop-Culture Magick*. Stafford, U.K.: Immanion Press/Magalithica Books, 2004.

Gribbin, John R. *The Jupiter Effect*. New York: Harper Collins, 1977.

———. *Beyond the Jupiter Effect*. Durham, U.K.: Macdonald Press, 1983.

Judith, Anodea. *Wheels of Life*. Audio recording with Rick Hamouris.

———. *The Illuminated Chakras*. DVD with Alex Wayne and Robin Silver.

Long, Max Freedom. *The Secret Science Behind Miracles*. Whitefish, Mont.: Kessinger, 2006.

———. *Recovering the Ancient Magic*. Whitefish, Mont.: Kessinger, 2005.

Moran, Elizabeth, and Val Biktashev. *The Complete Idiot's Guide to Feng Shui*, New York: Alpha Books, 2005.

Radin, Dean. *The Conscious Universe: The Scientific Truth of Psychic Phenomena*. San Francisco, Calif.: HarperSanFrancisco, 1997.

Reich, Wilhelm. *The Mass Psychology of Fascism*. New York: Farrar, Straus and Giroux, 1980.

Reich, Wilhelm, and Mary Boyd Higgins. *Wilhelm Reich Selected Writings*. New York: Farrar, Straus and Giroux, 1961.

Sollars, David W. *The Complete Idiot's Guide to Acupuncture and Acupressure*. New York: Alpha Books, 2000.

Appendix B

Recommended Websites

These are sites that we think readers will find interesting, educational, and/or fun.

- ✦ American College of Orgonomy:
  www.orgonomy.org
- ✦ American Society for Psychical Research:
  www.aspr.com
- ✦ Anodea Judith:
  www.sacredcenters.com
- ✦ Blavatsky Study Center:
  www.blavatskyarchives.com
- ✦ Christopher Penczak:
  www.christopherpenczak.com
- ✦ Crystals: More Than Meets the Eye:
  www.cis.yale.edu / ynhti / pubs / A5 / vanwagner
- ✦ Findhorn Community:
  www.findhorn.com.
- ✦ Global Consciousness Project:
  www.noosphere.princeton.edu

- ✦ Glossary of Frequently Misused or Misunderstood Physics Terms and Concepts: *www.lhup.edu/~dsimanek/glossary*
- ✦ Insider's Guide to Body Therapies: *www.learn-massage-online.com*
- ✦ Institute of Noetic Sciences: *www.noetic.org.*
- ✦ Internet Sacred Text Archive: *www.sacred-texts.com*
- ✦ Isaac and Phaedra Bonewits: *www.neopagan.net*
- ✦ Jose Silva UltraMind System: *www.silvaultramindsystem*
- ✦ KirlianResearch.com: *www.kirlianresearch.com*
- ✦ New Age Dictionary: *www.mysticplanet.com/8diction*
- ✦ Oberon & Morning Glory Zell-Ravenheart: *www.mythicimages.com*
- ✦ Parapsychological Association: *www.parapsych.org*
- ✦ Parapsychology Foundation: *www.parapsychology.org*
- ✦ Rhine Research Center: *www.rhine.org*
- ✦ Sacred Texts: *www.sacred-texts.com*
- ✦ The Witches' Voice: *www.witchvox.com*
- ✦ Uri Geller: *www.uri-geller.com*
- ✦ Venkman Test: *www.michaelthompson.org/venkman*
- ✦ Willow Polson: *www.willowsplace.com*

Appendix C

Science and Scientism

(Note: This extract is from *Authentic Thaumaturgy*.)

When examining mystical, magical, or parapsychological ideas we must first take down some barriers to clear thinking of which many people are unaware. Discussing metaphysical matters with modern Westerners, even those religiously inclined, is often like discussing rainbows or sunsets with someone who has worn dark sunglasses for his or her entire life. First you must persuade them to remove the sunglasses, at least temporarily, in order to show them what you are talking about. This is especially difficult if the person is unaware that the sunglasses exist, or that they can be removed. Unless you have carefully prepared them for the experience, the odds are high that their reaction to an unfiltered rainbow or sunset will be to scream in horror, replace their sunglasses as quickly as possible, and attack you violently.

Jewish, Christian, or Islamic fundamentalists trying to prevent evolution from being taught in public schools, or burning the works of heretical authors, or insisting on theocratic legal systems being given equal or superior power to secular ones, all demonstrate this common Western reaction to ideas coming from outside of their established worldviews. What may not be so obvious is that third-rate stage magicians and mediocre scientists 'debunking' evidence for psychic phenomena, intellectual members of liberal religions ignoring the magical aspects of worship rituals, or ordinary people rejecting ideas about magical or psychic phenomena, are behaving in exactly the same fashion—prisoners of the conceptual sunglasses they don't even realize they are wearing.

Three centuries of modern science have devastated so many old interpretations of the monotheistic traditions about the origins and development of life and other matters that many intelligent, educated Westerners have, consciously or not, decided that all monotheistic beliefs are equally "unscientific." Yet a person who has rejected every other monotheistic dogma of their childhood will often continue to accept the one that says Judaism/Christianity/Islam (choose one, and then a denomination within it) is the only "real" religion, and all others are foolish, weak, or demonic. This, of course, is based on the conservative monotheistic belief that there's only One God, only One Reality, and therefore only One True Religion—theirs!

Yet once you have decided that the only "real" religion (your childhood one) is "unscientific," and therefore "unworthy of belief" by a modern intellectual, it's a short step to declaring all those other "inferior" religions, magical systems, and psychic technologies to be even more unscientific and absurd. The philosophical term for this type of logic is "throwing out the baby with the bathwater." The usual result is a conversion to atheism, agnosticism, or some other non-theistic (but still dualistic) faith.

One of the most popular choices is Scientism (also known as "Scientolatry" and "Secular Humanism"), which is the worship of the previous generation's (sometimes the nineteenth century's) scientific worldview. People who are devout followers of Scientism share a number of dogmas, the most important of which is the one that they don't have any. These people will always declare themselves to be open-minded and willing to be convinced of the error of their ways—and then set up the logical rules of their game to exclude all non-Scientistic reasoning or evidence as fallacious. That's because there's only one reality, and only one way to understand it—does this sound familiar? Of course, it's exactly the same tactic followed by religious fundamentalists who insist that all "evidence" and "logic" must fit with their scripture's definitions of truth and its circular reasoning patterns—always a no-win game for the competing belief system.

Scientism is dualistic, just like the conservative monotheistic philosophies from which it is descended (via the medieval Christian and Islamic universities). All statements are Absolutely True or Absolutely False, except in the area of physics, where Scientistic types will usually—if reluctantly—admit the necessity of the "uncertainty principle," but insist that it only applies to subatomic phenomena. Because of their basic fear of ambiguity (which many feminist philosophers believe is rooted in fear of the feminine) and their frustration with a universe that does not actually fit into nice, neat, little pigeon-holes, Scientistic people are terrified of parapsychology, mysticism, and magic. They react to claims of paranormal activity, not with the lofty intellectual neutrality they brag about, but with the same anger, hatred, and fear that fundamentalists of other religions express when confronted with "counterfeit miracles" (those done by members of competing faiths), and for the same psychological and theological reasons. To the followers of Scientism, all miracles are counterfeit, and always will be, world without end, amen. Any experiments they set up to test alleged miracles will always—surprise!—wind up producing the answers they expect to see.

Scientism should not be confused with genuine science. Science is a collection of intellectual tools, organized into various systems known as "scientific methods" (there are many), each of which is designed to discover and organize certain types of knowledge (physics, chemistry, biology, sociology, anthropology, and so on). The methods of the so-called "hard" or "physical" sciences are not very useful for understanding music, poetry, love, religion, bliss, or other important aspects of human experience (that's what the "soft" or "social" sciences are supposedly for). Of course, superior scientists seldom claim that the methods of any one system of science are universally applicable.[1] It's primarily the mediocre scientists, who are more frightened than inspired by the unknown, who try to insist that (their particular) "Science is the Answer" to every single question that a human can ask.

Unfortunately, most people in our dualistic culture are unable to tell the difference between real science and Scientism, or between healthy skepticism and unhealthy cynicism for that matter, and this includes many with strong interests in spiritual matters both inside and outside of the Neopagan, New Age, or Spiritualist communities, who often assume that all outsiders calling themselves scientists will be hostile and dogmatic.

The irony is that, although it's true the hard sciences don't really support conservative monotheistic doctrines anymore, over the last fifty years all the sciences have tended more and more towards multi-model, pluralistic theories that fit very well indeed with many traditional concepts of polytheistic or unorthodox spirituality. This makes it sad that even people who have consciously rejected conservative monotheism are reluctant to let go of certain Scientistic prejudices, especially those concerning materialism and the nature of reality.

On the other paw, and it's a big one, many real scientists are driven to distraction by the ways that non-scientists misuse terms and ideas from mainstream sciences and technologies to describe how they think various metaphysical, mystical, magical, and psychic phenomena seem to behave. As we saw in this book, every generation of people interested in such "damned" (as Charles Fort called them) facts has attempted to 'explain' what they thought was going on in terms that would at least sound scientific or scholarly. These often produced what seem to be ludicrous results to later generations, who know that they have the peak of scientific knowledge and terminology that should be properly applied, and are themselves laughed at generations later.

As people interested in matters of a mystical nature, we need to not be intimidated or bamboozled by Scientistic debunkers, while remaining open to working with genuine scientists. That's what groups like the Institute of Noetic Sciences or the Parapsychology Association are for.

Notes

Introduction

1. This should not be confused with the mundane use of "polarization," which refers to a philosophical or political movement toward dualistic extremes.

2. From *www.groups.yahoo.com/group/cuups-café*, accessed 1/10/07. All comments attributed to the Physics Police came from personal correspondence with the authors, or via the CUUPS e-list.

Chapter 1

1. Which then powers the computers that control the Stargate so it can open a stable wormhole through multidimensional space to the Pegasus Galaxy, using the Zero Point Module as its power source—but that's getting way too advanced for this book.

2. This is sometimes believed to be a cosmically distributed force, as in *Star Wars*, and/or an omnipresent deity.

3. Posted on CUUPS Café. Accessed 1/10/07.

4. Girl electron: "Do we turn right or left at the nucleus?"
   Boy electron: "Don't worry, I know the way!"

5. From a personal communication received from William Seligman on 8/31/06.

6. For more on the various percentages of dark matter and dark energy, see "The Universe's Invisible Hand" by Christopher J. Conselice, published in *Scientific American*, February, 2007.

7. Some graduate student somewhere could probably get a Ph.D. out of analyzing Eddy's writings for evidence of her being an abuse survivor.

8. If you do much reading of Western esoteric books you will find an almost universal need to appeal to the "authority" of the ancient Egyptians (and the mythical Atlanteans).

9. Taken from part s of Chapters 2 and 3 of *The Kybalion*, found on *www.sacred-texts.com*. Accessed 1/15/07.

Chapter 2

1. From *Real Magic*, pg. 258.

2. From *Rites of Worship*, pp. 16–18. For more on this, see *Real Magic* and Chapter 7 of this book.

3. See *Real Magic* and *Rites of Worship* for more details on these topics.

4. Members of mystical—and usually dualistic—movements in the eastern Mediterranean countries during the years 400 B.C.E. to 400 C.E., who strongly affected the development of Christianity.

5. Selected extracts taken from *Rites of Worship*, pp. 32–35.

6. See *Real Magic* for more details on ritual.

7. Perhaps the connection is tunneling through a wormhole in subspace.

8. "Stay the course!"

9. Scientism treats science as a collection of dogmas to be memorized, as in the modern American elementary and high school education. See Appendix D.

10. *The Pagan Man.*

11. Phaedra says, "Sure, why not? It's no wackier than a lot of the other stuff I've been reading for this book!"

Chapter 3

1. See *Bonewits's Essential Guide to Druidism* for a more detailed discussion of this.

2. Ibid.

3. Others have been known to claim that the fifth Element is really Pet Hair, but scientists disagree as non-pet-owning scientists have been unable to replicate the observations of those who are pet owners.

4. This idea comes from Aristotle. See Figure 12.

5. From *The Magus*, pp. 73–74. This ties in to Barrett's discussion of astrology, with each Element making three signs "cardinal," "fixed," or "mutable," and giving rise to the modern Western zodiac of 12 signs.

6. From *The Way of Four*, pg. 3.

7. This is a reference to spontaneous generation, now known to be false.

8. From *The Magus*, pp. 76–77.One of many references to alchemy.

9. In the non-Aristotelian sense.

10. From *The Way of Four*, pg.9.

11. From *The Magus*, pg. 77.

12. From *The Way of Four*, pp. 7–8.

13. Perhaps a reference to the pheromones (molecules of odor) released at death?

14. From *The Magus*, pg. 79.

15. Ibid., 81.

16. From *The Way of Four*, pg. 6.

17. From *The Magus*, pp. 75–76.

18. Other than the rules that are known by fire fighters and physicists.

19. From *The Way of Four*, pg. 6.

Chapter 4

1. Does anyone still use clock hands, or do we need to say "when Mr. Digital reads 12:00"?

2. Not the constellation Aries. Astrological timekeeping has gradually moved away from astronomical timekeeping, due to something called the "precession of the equinoxes."

3. As shown in Chapter 5, Chinese astrology is very different.

4. The idea that deities could be pigeonholed into having only a small number of areas of interest or influence was exaggerated by the Homeric poets, who gave us the Twelve Olympians of ancient Greek myth.

5. One stone was missing for many years, leading to criticism about the fact that the sun didn't rise directly over the one that remained. However, archeologists have recently found the pit where a stone of equal size to the remaining one would have been placed, just as Isaac had predicted many years ago.

6. They looked like little "Reddy Kilowatt" figures, for those old enough to remember them.

7. Your esteemed authors do suspect that there are plenty of other authors, ritualists, and workshop leaders who don't have a clue themselves as to how to ground or center; they just know when you're supposed to tell people to do it!

Chapter 5

1. Lao-tzu. *Tao Te Ching* (Translation by Stephen Mitchell). New York, N.Y.: HarperCollins, 1988.

2. Sollars, David. *The Complete Idiot's Guide to Acupuncture & Acupressure.* New York, N.Y.: Alpha Books, 2000.

Chapter 6

1. Except perhaps for the folly of walking around with a rock tied to your arm by an ass's hair?

2. From *The Magus*, pp. 39–40.

3. Throughout this book, we will use the name "God" in the singular to denote the traditional Western concept of a Supreme Being with various anthropomorphic aspects, combined with the liberal theology common to mystics and heretics.

4. A little spindle that allows the stone on the ring to be turned toward or away from the finger.

5. A spiritually focused magician, remember?

6. But stay away from his computer!

7. From *The Secret Teachings of All Ages*, pg. 100.

8. Taken from an online article titled "Liber 777 on the Cheap" (copyright 1979), by Frater AMTh, at *www.totse.com/en/religion/pagans_and_wiccans/stones.html*. Accessed 1/15/07.

9. See his *Magick in Theory and Practice.*

10. Kids, ask your parents.

11. "The Science of Crystal Healing," by Crystal Healer. Found at *www.indianreikimasters.com/crystalhealing*. Accessed 01/15/07.

12. From *The Crystal Wisdom Book*, pg. 9.

13. Ibid., pg. 12.

14. Ibid., pg. 101.

15. From *Healing With Crystals and Chakra Energies*, pg. 69.

16. For an excellent discussion of this by three such people, see *www.floweressencemagazine.com / nov02 / doctrineofsignatures*.

17. From *The Magus*, pg. 29.

18. From *The Secret Teachings of All Ages*, pg. 93. There are also medieval and Renaissance books that seem to recommend using different body parts; these are actually references to plants that resemble those body parts.

19. According to Wikipedia, "Kirlian photography refers to a form of contact print photography, theoretically associated with high-voltage. It is named after Semyon Kirlian, who in 1939 accidentally discovered that if an object on a photographic plate is subjected to a strong electric field, an image is created on the plate." See *www.wikipedia.org / wiki / Kirlian_photography*.

20. From *The Magus*, pp. 37–38.

21. From *The Druid Animal Oracle Deck*, pg. 10.

22. From *The Sociology of Furry Fandom,* by David J. Rust. See *www.visi.com / ~phantos / furrysoc*.

Chapter 7

1. Note: this word has a different and more technical meaning in the field of psychology. Some authors who write about psychic phenomenon or fantasy role-playing (FRP) games equate psychometry with clairtangency.

Chapter 8

1. See his *The Secret Science Behind Miracles, The Secret Science at Work*, and *The Huna Code in Religions* for details.

2. See Isaac's *Bonewits's Essential Guide to Witchcraft and Wicca* for details on how Gardner accomplished this with Wicca.

3. For more on medical astrology as practiced today, see *How to Give an Astrological Health Reading,* by Diane L. Cramer.

4. Moran, Elizabeth, and Val Biktashev. *The Complete Idiot's Guide to Feng* Shui. New York, N.Y.: Alpha Books, 1999.

5. We highly recommend all her works on these topics, including her classic book *Wheels of Life,* her audio recording *Wheels of Life: A Journey Through the Chakras* (with Rick Hamouris), and her DVD *The Illuminated Chakras* (with Alex Wayne and Robin Silver). Her website is *www.sacredcenters.com*.

Chapter 9
1. From *Rites of Worship*, pg. 20.
2. Deborah Lipp has a great deal of useful information and advice about Elementals in her book, *The Elements of Ritual.*
3. As for the so-called Fairy Traditions of Wicca, consult *Bonewits's Essential Guide to Witchcraft and Wicca* for a brief history of their riotous variety.
4. A bit of a hellraiser, but a good occultist.
5. See *Kingdom of the Gods,* by Geoffrey Hodson.
6. See *www.findhorn.com.*
7. Quoting the 2007 version of the essay at *www.neopagan.net/NeopagansBelieve.* Accessed 1/10/07.
8. From *The Druid Chronicles (Evolved),* by the Reformed Druids of North America. Privately printed, and available online at *www.student.carleton.edu/orgs/druids/ARDA.* Accessed 1/10/07.

Chapter 10
1. From *Rites of Worship*, pp. 191–192.
2. Modified somewhat from *Rites of Worship.*
3. See *Rites of Worship* for a detailed discussion of public worship rituals.
4. We probably don't need to point out to many of our readers that the metaphysics of the *Star Wars* universe is essentially sci-fi Taoism, but for the rest of you, we just did (although that garbage George Lucas came up with about mitaclorians was absolute nonsense).
5. From *Rites of Worship*, pg. 198.

Chapter 11
1. We suppose you could create some kind of air blast that might do the job, but it would wear away the steel with friction and destroy it.

Appendix C
1. You can, however, manage to get Nobel Prize winners who know little about a given subject, such as astrology, to publicly denounce all of it as "superstition," usually at the behest of Scientistic debunkers.

Bibliography

We have read several thousand books between the two of us, many of which were read so long ago that neither of us can remember specific titles. The following list is comprised of the works that were directly consulted during the writing process, but it does not represent all of the books that effectively contributed to this work.

Barrett, Francis. *The Magus: A Complete System of Occult Philosophy*. York Beach, Maine: Weiser Books, 2000.

Blavatsky, Helena Petrovna. *The Secret Doctrine*. Pasadena, Calif.: Theosophical University Press, 1999.

———. *Isis Unveiled*. Pasadena, Calif.: Theosophical University Press, 1999.

Bonewits, Isaac. *Real Magic: An Introductory Treatise on the Basic Principles of Yellow Magic*. York Beach, Maine: Weiser Books, 1989.

———. *Authentic Thaumaturgy*. Austin, Tex.: Steve Jackson Games, 1998.

———. *Rites of Worship: A Neopagan Approach*. El Sobrante, Calif.: Earth Religions Press, 2003.

————. *The Pagan Man: Priests, Warriors, Hunters, and Drummers.* New York: Citadel, 2005.

Brennan, Barbara Ann. *Hands of Light.* New York: Bantam Books, 1988.

Bulwer-Lytton, Edward. *Vril, The Power of the Coming Race.* Rockville, Md.: Wildside Press, 2002.

Carr-Gomm, Philip and Stephanie. *The Druid Animal Oracle Deck.* New York: Simon and Shuster, 1994.

Crowley, Aleister. *777 and Other Qabalistic Writings of Aleister Crowley.* York Beach, Maine: Weiser Books, 1986.

Gray, William G. *Magical Ritual Methods.* York Beach, ME: Weiser Books, 1980.

Greene, Brian. *The Elegant Universe: Superstrings, Hidden Dimensions, and the Quest for the Ultimate Theory.* New York: Vintage Books, 2000.

Hall, Manly P. *The Secret Teachings of All Ages.* New York: Tarcher, 2003.

Harrison, Stephanie and Barbara Kleiner. *The Crystal Wisdom Book.* North Clarendon, Vt.: Journey Editions, 1997.

Hodson, Geoffrey. *Kingdom of the Gods.* Whitefish, Mont.: Kessinger, 2003.

Hoffman, Enid. *Huna: A Beginner's Guide.* Atglen, Pa.: Whitford Press, 1976.

Holzner, Steve. *Physics for Dummies.* Hoboken, NJ: Wiley, 2004.

Hopman, Ellen Evert. *Tree Medicine Tree Magic.* West Kennebunk, Maine: Phoenix, 1991.

————. *A Druid's Herbal for the Sacred Earth Year.* Rochester, Vt.: Destiny Books, 1994.

Judith, Anodea. *Wheels of Life.* Woodbury, Minn.: Llewellyn Worldwide, 1999.

Kardec, Allan. *The Spirits' Book.* New York: Cosimo, 2006.

————. *The Book on Mediums.* York Beach, ME: Weiser Books, 1989.

Kieth, William H. *The Science of the Craft*. New York: Citadel, 2005.

Lao-tzu. *Tao Te Ching*. Translation by Stephen Mitchell. New York: HarperCollins, 1988.

Lilly, Sue and Simon. *Healing with Crystals and Chakra Energies*. New York: Barnes and Noble Books, 2005.

Lipp, Deborah. *The Way of Four*. Woodbury, Minn.: Llewellyn Worldwide, 2002.

———. *The Elements of Ritual*. Woodbury, Minn.: Llewellyn Worldwide, 2003.

Michell, John F. *The New View Over Atlantis*. London/New York: Thames & Hudson, 2001.

Radin, Dean. *Entangled Minds: Extrasensory Experiences in a Quantum Reality*. New York: Paraview Pocket Books, 2006.

Reich, Wilhelm. *The Function of the Orgasm: Discovery of the Orgone*. New York: Farrar, Straus and Giroux, 1986.

The Three Initiates. *The Kybalion: A Study of the Hermetic Philosophy of Ancient Egypt and Greece*. Chicago, Ill.: Yoga Publication Society, 1998.

von Reichenbach, Karl. *Researches on Magnetism, Electricity, Heat, Light Crystalization and Chemical Attraction in Relation to the Vital Force*. Isle of Arran, UK: Banton Press, 1998.

White, John, and Stanley Krippner. *Future Science*. New York: Anchor Books, 1977.

Wilson, Robert Anton. *Cosmic Trigger I*. Tempe, Ariz.: New Falcon Publications, 1991.

The Shorter Oxford English Dictionary, Fifth Edition. Oxford, UK: Oxford University Press, 2002.

Index

About the Authors

ISAAC BONEWITS was the first student to graduate with a bachelor's degree in magic from an accredited university. He has been present at many of the most historical events in the American Neo-Pagan community. He is the author of numerous books, and is probably the best-known representative of the modern Druid revival in North America. He is also a Wiccan, was active in Aleister Crowley's order of Ceremonial Magic (the OTO), and has been initiated into Santeria.

PHAEDRA BONEWITS has been a practicing occultist for about 30 years. She has been initiated into Hermetic Magic and several forms of modern witchcraft, and has close working relationships with practitioners of such paths as Ifa and Druidism. She had the opportunity to experience firsthand the application of the energetic theories of oriental medicine, even serving as a body model for a shiatsu course.

They live in Rockland County, New York, with Isaac's part-time resident son, Arthur, and two cats that are active in the war against literacy.

Books of Related Interest

➤ *Creating Circles & Ceremonies*
Oberon and Morning Glory Zell-Ravenheart
EAN 978-1-56414-864-3

➤ *Magickal Connections*
Lisa Mc Sherry
EAN 978-1-56414-932-9

➤ *The Mysteries of Druidry*
Brendan Cathbad Myers
EAN 978-1-56414-878-0

➤ *Soul Sex*
Pala Copeland and Al Link
EAN 978-1-56414-664-9

➤ *Exploring Reiki*
Dr. Laxmi Paula Horan
EAN 978-1-56414-823-0

◆

New Page Books
P.O. Box 687
Franklin Lakes, NJ 07417
1-800-227-3371
www.NewPageBooks.com